Helping Children
Cope with Death

Helping Children Cope with Death
Guidelines and Resources

Edited by
HANNELORE WASS
University of Florida, Gainesville
and
CHARLES A. CORR
Southern Illinois University, Edwardsville

⬤ HEMISPHERE PUBLISHING CORPORATION
Washington   New York   London

DISTRIBUTION OUTSIDE THE UNITED STATES
McGRAW–HILL INTERNATIONAL BOOK COMPANY
Auckland   Bogotá   Guatemala   Hamburg   Johannesburg
Lisbon   London   Madrid   Mexico   Montreal
New Delhi   Panama   Paris   San Juan   São Paulo
Singapore   Sydney   Tokyo   Toronto

HELPING CHILDREN COPE WITH DEATH: Guidelines and Resources

2 3 4 5 6 7 8 9 0   B R B R   8 9 8 7 6 5 4 3 2

This book was set in Baskerville by Hemisphere Publishing Corporation.
The editors were Christine Flint and Janet Mais; the production supervisor
was Miriam Gonzalez and the typesetter was Shirley J. McNett.
Braun-Brumfield, Inc., was printer and binder.

Library of Congress Cataloging in Publication Data

Helping children cope with death.

(Series in death education, aging, and health care)
"Audiovisual resources": p.
Bibliography: p.
Includes index.
1. Children and death. I. Wass, Hannelore. II. Corr,
Charles A. III. Series.
BF723.D3H44   155.9'37   81-20221
ISBN 0-89116-247-X   AACR2
ISSN 0275-3510

To
BRIAN,
KEVIN,
KAREN,
and SUSAN

CONTENTS

CONTRIBUTORS

Sandra L. Bertman, M.A.
Associate Professor, Program of Ethics, Values, and Medical Humanities,
University of Massachusetts Medical School, Worcester, Massachusetts

Charles A. Corr, Ph.D.
Professor, Philosophical Studies, School of Humanities,
Southern Illinois University at Edwardsville, Edwardsville, Illinois

Edgar N. Jackson, Ph.D.
Minister, Writer, and Consultant, Washington Road, Corinth, Vermont

Richard A. Pacholski, Ph.D.
Professor and Chairman, Department of English,
Millikin University, Decatur, Illinois

Hannelore Wass, Ph.D.
Professor, Educational Psychology and Human Development,
Department of Foundations of Education, University of Florida,
Gainesville, Florida

∞∞

PREFACE

∞∞

As more and more parents, teachers, and other adults face up to the pressing need to help our young cope with death, it becomes apparent that guidelines and resources for effective helping are also needed. In this supplementary volume we have attempted to provide these.

Part One of our book, Guidelines, consists of three chapters. In the chapter by Sandra Bertman, the reader can see some of the richness of children's relationships with the phenomenon of death and some stunning verbal and artistic expressions of their death concerns. The chapter also gives illustrations of the sensitivity to children's needs found in the creative literature. Edgar Jackson shares insights he has gained from counseling children. He suggests specific ways in which a counselor, especially a pastoral counselor, can help, and offers a set of basic guidelines for effective counseling. Both chapters may stimulate the reader to explore further the considerable wealth of knowledge that now exists about death and the child. Charles Corr not only presents a carefully reasoned discussion of opportunities and responsibilities for death education, but also deals with the complex question of goals; he suggests a variety of forms that death education for children can take and ways in which various resources can be used effectively.

In Part Two of our volume we offer a comprehensive listing of a variety of resources that we consider helpful for those who want to be effective helpers. Here Charles Corr presents an annotated bibliography of 44 books for adults. Hannelore Wass provides an annotated bibliography of 156 books about death for children and adolescents. Richard Pacholski provides an annotated mediagraphy consisting of 136 entries.

We hope this volume will be useful to parents, teachers, counselors, and other adults who interact with children.

Hannelore Wass and Charles A. Corr

INTRODUCTION

HANNELORE WASS AND CHARLES A. CORR

In his oft-quoted book, *The Prophet,* Kahlil Gibran says: "If you would indeed behold the spirit of death, open your heart wide unto the body of life. For life and death are one, even as the river and the sea are one" (1, p. 80). This insight is fundamental and many writers have expressed it in various ways. To the extent that we are able to gain insight into the meaning of death before it actually comes to us individually, we must do so through an understanding of life. That is not so unusual, for the human condition as we know it is to have to view things from the perspective of the only life that we now have to live. Further, an appreciation of transitoriness and finitude, of separation and loss within life, is one way of approximating the final cessation and limitation of life. And much of what we commonly speak of as "death" is really a mode of *living* that immediately precedes or follows that event. For example, references to the "death" of a person often actually concern his or her *dying,* and comments about difficulties with the "death" of a spouse may actually have to do with the mate's *bereavement.* Thus, as Gibran tells us, the correct approach to a human understanding of death is properly seen as a study of life in all of its fullness.

This is worth mentioning because it is sometime suggested that learning about death is a kind of extraordinary or odd adventure. On the contrary, learning about death is actually at the same time learning about life. This is to repeat Gibran's observation and also to bring into focus its obverse. As argued elsewhere:

> On the one hand, death will be thought to be unimportant wherever we lack the imagination or the sensitivity to see and to

1

feel the importance of life. And on the other hand, by distancing ourselves from death and losing respect for its significance, we also find ourselves drawing away from a sense of the value of life. (2, p. 37)

We cannot grasp or evaluate correctly the proportions and the significance of life if we do not bring death into the picture. Just as death must be construed through life, so also life must eventaully be seen in the context of death. Certainly, death is not the only perspective from which to understand life. But it is an essential one, and in the long run, it is indispensable as a constitutive element of human existence. That is why death can become, as Herman Feifel once said, a "piloting force" in our lives. Consistently to keep death out of an account of life is to misperceive our human mode of being in a way that is fundamental and not otherwise correctable.

Acknowledging that death and life are inextricably intertwined need not, however, be an exercise of daily confrontation. In fact, many of us race, hurdle, or stumble through each day, often overwhelmed by the moment-to-moment demands of living, imprisoned by routine and endless detail, worried about tasks unfinished and plans yet to be realized. But it is imperative that every so often we take time out to look back, look forward, and look within in order to move beyond the current moment and discover or rediscover the larger picture. Often it takes a personal crisis such as a death to force us to stop and ponder in this way. Many times a child's probing questions are the impetus for us to reflect on meanings and purposes in life and death.

For today's children, death is more remote than ever before. During the 19th century and the early part of the 20th, the experience of a death in the family was common to children. Most witnessed the death of at least one sibling, and many before reaching adulthood also lost one or both parents. Because most people died at home, children were intimately acquainted with all aspects of dying. They often helped care for the dying family member, witnessed the moment of death, and participated in the funeral. Thus, children lived with the fact of death from infancy and there was nothing strange about it. With rapid advances in medical science and technology, infant mortality has been drastically reduced; many infectious diseases have been conquered to a large degree; and many others can be cured. As a consequence, average life expectancy has increased from about 47 years at the turn of the century to about 76 years today. In fact, the past two generations are the first in history in which many people in our society have reached middle age without having experienced the death of a close family member (3).

As *direct* personal experience with death has become more limited, *indirect* experience through the media, especially television, has vastly increased. The amounts of time children spend in front of a television set are unprecedented, and the extent of the impact of this medium is something with which we have to reckon. We know as yet relatively little about the long-range effect that television may have on our young, but early indications are that its influence may be formidable. There is at least one television set in 98 percent of American households, and children are television's heaviest users (4). The view of death presented by television programs is highly distorted. Often death is portrayed as something that does not happen at all. For example, Wiley Coyote on "Road Runner" gets tossed into a ravine, shot, stabbed, blown up, and run over—yet he instantly returns to life and the chase resumes. In "The Bionic Man" and "The Bionic Woman," two ordinary people become practically indestructible because they are superhuman in strength and endurance. When death does occur on television, it is often without visible pain, blood, or tears. Most television deaths are the result of violent acts; few people die a natural death; honest bereavement is rarely depicted; and actors who have long been dead are frequently resurrected through reruns. What notions of the nature of dying and death can a child glean from such exposure? Obviously it will be up to adults to make certain that such misperceptions are replaced with facts. Psychologists and educators are urging parents to seek a better balance for their children between fantasized portraits of death on television and direct personal experience or constructive accounts in literature.

Parents and teachers are important people in the lives of children. Raising and educating a child is a great responsibility and challenge. Even though this is often a joyful and gratifying venture, we are sometimes reminded of how awesome a task it is. There is no denying the fact that our responsibilities on behalf of children are difficult. They require continued goodwill, genuine caring, and personal maturity, along with knowledge of the child's world and a deep sensitivity to the child's needs. Though all of us were once children, it is all too easy to forget what that was like. And it is difficult at one and the same time to carry out our adult responsibilities and to put ourselves in the child's place. Nevertheless, this is what we must be able to do to be most effective in helping the child grow and develop in a healthy manner.

If we want to help children understand and interpret direct or indirect death-related experiences, if we want to help alleviate fears and provide comfort for children, we need to know something of their thoughts and feelings about death. But this immediately presents obstacles for many of us. First of all, the terms *children* and *death* seem contradictory. To associate them seems to violate our sense of appropriateness. Children symbolize life and growth and the future, whereas death marks decay, the end of growing, and what is now past. Bringing the two together seems morbid. But death is a natural part of life, a dimension with special power to help us appreciate the preciousness of life. When we realize this and free ourselves from misguided thinking, we will have overcome the primary obstacle. The second obstacle is also difficult to overcome. It concerns our natural tendency to shield and protect our children. We want to shield children from the harsh reality of death and thereby from frightening thoughts about death. The problem is that, no matter how hard we may try to do this, in the long run we cannot. Perhaps we can for a while, but as children grow older we cannot control and restrict their experiences. Indeed, we might ask: Should we even try? Mental health specialists have long noted that overprotection is as harmful to the child as neglect. Both stunt normal growth. Death is a natural and normal part of life. It creates fears and anxieties, but adults can comfort children and assist them to cope with such realities.

Other obstacles include misconceptions and erroneous notions about the thoughts and feelings that children have in relation to death. We need to overcome some common misunderstandings by using knowledge about both childhood and death—knowledge that has come from research and clinical observation over the last several decades. What are some of these misconceptions and what are some of the true facts? One common misconception holds that children are not interested in death, and if they are, they need psychiatric care. This is not so. On the contrary, it is a sign of normal, healthy development when children want to know about death. Children have a need to know and understand themselves, others, and the world around them. Given the opportunity and a supportive, responsive atmosphere, children begin asking fundamental existential questions at a very early age. Often we adults do not recognize these questions for what they are. For example, the question Where do babies come from? or the more pointed question How are babies made? is, when asked by a very young child, often misinterpreted as an unhealthy and inappropriate interest in sex. Nothing could be further from the truth. The child is concerned with the origin of her or his existence. Such questions are in the same category as: What are we before we are born? Are we air or dust or ants? Where are we before we are born? Or these questions: Why do people die? What happens when people die? Where do you go when you are dead? These are all quite proper and natural questions about the basic meaning of life and death that are likely to arise in childhood.

A related misconception is that children do not think about death on their own. Thus, unless we tell them, they will not have any idea about what death is. Wrong again. Through numerous studies conducted over a period of more than 40 years, we know that children's understandings of death depend to a large extent on their level of cognitive development, their experiences, and their perception of events in the world. Further, we know that children's thinking is qualitatively different from that of adults and that concepts of death usually develop in an orderly sequence. This sequence proceeds from nonconceptualization of death in infancy; to the concept in late infancy and early childhood that death is a reversible event, a temporary restriction, departure, or sleep; to the comprehension during middle childhood and preadolescence that death is irreversible but capricious; to the understanding during adolescence that death is irreversible, universal, and personal but distant. These concepts develop in close relation to a child's experiences. Today's child may not be exposed to the death of a close family member, but there are other deaths that may occur, such as the death of a relative, a neighbor, and sometimes a classmate. Most frequently, however, the child comes into contact with death through animals. These experiences touch off many questions that deserve honest answers. Being kept in the dark creates its own anxieties. In addition, if we adults hedge and evade such questions, we unintentionally communicate a powerful message to the child: "Death is such a horrible thing that it terrifies even adults so much that they can't talk about it." Such unspoken communication only intensifies perplexity and anxiety.

The misconceptions that we have mentioned lead logically to the mistaken belief that children do not have any fears of anxieties about death. The facts do not bear out this belief. Fears and anxieties develop early in infancy and take on many forms. The earliest fears are those that threaten the infant's survival, the fear of being separated from or abandoned by the nurturing one. Variations of this fear are fears associated with being left alone, not recognizing a familiar face, or being in a dark place. Young children have many fears that are related to personal danger. They fear monsters, wild animals, witches, ghosts. They worry about the dead being unable to breathe or to get out from under the ground when they wake up. As children's concepts of death become more realistic and children mature, death-related fears become increasingly more like those of adults.

There are a number of good sources of information related to children's death fears and anxieties. They are listed in Part II of this volume in the annotated bibliographies of books for adults and audiovisual resources. Much of what is written can be helpful to parents, teachers, counselors, and other adults as basic background information. But we must remember that each child is unique; to help a particular child cope with fears and anxieties, we must try to listen to this particular child with a "third ear," as Wilhelm Reich has suggested. By that, he means that we must be sensitive and tuned in to a child's thoughts, feelings, and actions. No adult will find comprehensive answers that will be universally valid for all children. But each can develop specific responses to individual needs in a process of personalized sharing with his or her child. Helping children in this way to cope with death in life more effectively is a worthwhile, rewarding, and challenging task. With that in mind we have attempted in this little book to alert adults to special needs of children, to offer guidelines for effective helping, and to direct attention to resources that can assist in that undertaking.

References

1. Gibran, K. *The Prophet.* New York: Knopf, 1972.
2. Corr, C. Reconstructing the changing face of death. In H. Wass (Ed.), *Dying: Facing the facts.* Washington: Hemisphere, 1979, pp. 5–43.
3. Stillion, J., & Wass, H. Children and death. In H. Wass (Ed.), *Dying: Facing the facts.* Washington: Hemisphere, 1979, pp. 208–235.
4. Wass, H., & Cason, L. Death anxiety and fears in childhood. In H. Wass & C. A. Corr (Eds.), *Childhood and death.* Washington: Hemisphere, in press.

GUIDELINES

∞∞

CHILDREN'S AND OTHERS' THOUGHTS AND EXPRESSIONS ABOUT DEATH

∞∞

SANDRA L. BERTMAN

University of Massachusetts Medical Center, Worcester

Death: Some Definitions

Death is

"when a person can't live any longer"
"old age"
"when someone dies"

In other words, death is some sort of simple fact, biologically appropriate, with little psychological baggage attached.
    Death is

"when you go to another place or world"

That is, death is movement and transition.
    Death is

"someone dyeing [sic] and letting some room in the world
    for other living things"
"when God says it is time to leave"

That is, death is an interpretation of the scheme of the universe—orderly and according to a prexistent master plan.
    Death is

"when it doesn't hurt any more"

Death is, in other words, release from pain and suffering. Peace.

Death is

"when someone dies and all the people he knows come to
   see him buried [sic]"
"the spooks"

Death is, then, ritual, being the center of attention, connectedness, a being together, a time, scarey.
Death is,

"when you don't have to take tests and school"
"when everybody hates you"

Death is relief and excuse; better than failing, being friendless,
and feeling uncomfortable and alone.

These definitions from a class of fifth graders cover a range
of interpretations that smudge psychologically ascribed developmental lines (1, 2) both with their startling simplicity and with
their sophistication. The youngster's criteria are more than
biologic and clinical. They bespeak of continuum and human
values, such as relief from pain and suffering; find meaning by
merging with a universe in which life and death coexist; exhibit
a degree of comfort and trust and a sense of connection with all
humanity, future and past. Coexistent with the rational search
for reasons, explanations, and meaning about the event of death
are feelings of being scared, sad, angry, out of step, alone, and
"all wrong with the world." Such ideologies and sentiments have
been the subject matter of the most mature philosophers, poets,
and artists of any era.

Definitions are skeletal, limited, and limiting. When embel-
lishment is called for—through visual or verbal media—other
concerns surface. A major preoccupation appears to be the life
of the dead one, or the living dead. Specifics about the new
environment, the changed body, activities of the dead, and
connection with the living claim much attention. License for
fanciful thought tends to pummel one's darker imaginings and
fears. The more unmentionable concerns have to do with the
contagion of death, one's murderous impulses, fantasies using

the threat of death as a means of controlling others, and viewing death as punishment or as stigma.

Life of the Dead One

Children's literature attempts to address the concerns that youngsters express about life after death. In *Anne and the Sand Dobbies,* a father explains to younger siblings that their sister, Annie, is dead, but in residence elsewhere: "The simplest way to put it, I guess, is to say she's with God. Some people say she's in heaven. I don't know exactly where she is. All we know is that she is living and that she's all right—wherever she is" (3, p. 64). In *The Magic Moth,* a minister consoles the family with his belief that when people die they step through the door into another place the living cannot see with their eyes (4, p. 46). At another time, in this same book, an older sibling explains that, wherever her sister is, it is "nice" (4, p. 17).

The strict designation, the literal location of this heaven, is a subject of concern not just for the very young. The jests of Woody Allen, a 20th century comic philosopher, expose his (adult) underlying anxiety. He envisions heaven as a cocktail party but fears "no one will know where it is being held" (5). Quite the contrary, Emily Dickinson, a 19th-century poet, likens this uncharted place to moors or seas, neither of which she has actually experienced in her lifetime. In tones of faith and affirmation, she states the analogy:

I never spoke with God
nor visited in heaven
yet certain am I of the spot
as if the chart were given. (6, p. 201)

The "burid" body is not readily discarded by youngsters. In children's literature, adult characters explain that the body is tired, worn out, sick, outgrown. Death is the sloughing off of a useless husk. In *Thank You, Jackie Robinson,* this image is the consolation: "That's just Davy's shell, there in the box left behind like an old snake skin" (7, p. 115). The snake symbol of regeneration is appropos when one can witness the metamorphic process. The newly skinned snake literally slithers away. Unlike the snake, however, the whereabouts of the newly dead person— the one skinned, as it were—is less dramatically visible.

The cremated body is even harder to fathom. Visualizing Annie in heaven or with angels, without her intact body, is just not possible for the younger siblings: " 'But Annie hasn't got any arms at all, has she?' I asked. 'They're going to burn those arms off. They're going to burn her all up. Isn't that right, Dad? How can she fly if she hasn't got any arms?' " (3, p. 76).

Nine-year-olds have studied the question of what is dead. One youngster defined dead as "when your heart stops beating, when you stop breathing, and when you don't sneeze or hiccup any more" (8). A 12-year-old explained that the dead person continues to have a body, but without physical power. Yet this loss of physical power is paradoxical. For though the embodied spirit cannot taste, hear, or smell, it can hover and it can see. In this youngster's drawing (Fig. 1), depicting a ghost approximately four months after death, the spirit is envisioned "hover-[ing] over the family member of it's choice . . . but once it's chosen the person it can't leave until the member has died . . . the 'ghost,' then, can't really communicate with the living until s/he, too, dies" (9). The dead body still is quite corporeal— clothed as in life, watching, hovering near by, patiently waiting

FIGURE 1

to communicate more directly and reunite when the living member subsequently dies.

The spirit of the dead watching, however, can be spooky. In *The Rock and the Willow,* Leeroy, following a chastisement about his behavior, wonders if his dead mama can see him (10, p. 158). Such rituals as holding one's nose when passing cemeteries or not walking on burial plots bespeak belief in goblins who are waiting to get one if one does not watch out. Even the young artist of this picture admonishes that usually you close your ears and eyes and hold your breath—"you try to block off all your senses. You think a dead person may come to haunt you if you have a sense left open, so to speak" (9). One is reminded of Gauguin's painting *The Spirit of the Dead Watching* (11, p. 76), in which a spirit is portrayed as a black-hooded figure seated at the foot of a bed. A female figure lying on the bed faces the opposite direction—avoiding the spirit. Is the live young woman distressed by or simply unaware of the deceased's presence? Is she turned away, deliberately, trying to hide from death? Would she be comforted if she faced the shrouded one, acknowledging death's presence?

In *Little Women,* Beth, the one dying, tries, with her courage at giving up life, to comfort her sister Jo. Her faith, however, is pierced when she admits the hardest part is leaving her family. To her assurances that she is not afraid and that she will be taken care of by God, Beth adds poignantly, "but it seems that I should be homesick for you even in heaven" (12, p. 339). In *A Taste of Blackberries,* the child-narrator looks at the clouds ("horses and lambs and floppy-eared dogs chased across the sky") (13, p. 36) and wonders whether his dead friend is playing with them or being lonesome in heaven. Even for the dead, then, it would seem being alone is the worst curse imaginable.

In *Anne and the Sand Dobbies,* the father, though adding a new dimension of saintliness to being dead, nonetheless views the afterlife in terms of the activities and values of the human framework as we know it: "One thing I do know . . . is that you can't be a lone wolf in heaven. . . . You can't even be a lone wolf here. . . . When you're in heaven you just do this perfectly all the time rather than in the half-baked way we do it here" (3, pp. 75–76).

The dead, then, are felt to be altered but very much alive. They exist somewhere and function somehow, living almost as usual in a different place. Perhaps they are drinking cocktails à la Woody Allen or being decent like Annie, or lonesome like Beth or Jamie, or goblin ghosts. Life may be diminished for them—less than it was when "alive"; some senses do not work; routines are certainly different. But "out-of-body" in whatever sense, the essence and presence of the one dead is strongly felt by the living. Annie's ashes are buried near the summer beach house where the family had its happiest time together. Annie now lives in a spiritual world where, like the sand dobbies who are invisible, she does not *do* anything, she just *is:* "Seeing sand dobbies is the same as being able to see people because they have bodies. But even when you can't see their bodies anymore, the sand-dobby part of them, the *real* part still goes on" (3, pp. 108–109).

The child-narrator of *A Taste of Blackberries* ultimately comes to feel that his dead friend Jamie, too, was glad "the main sadness was over." He wonders how fast "angels" or "whatever he was now" can move, as he continues to play with his dislocated friend. "Race you," he calls to Jamie as he runs up the hill (13, p. 75).

Ghosts are the external sense of presence. In another sense, they are an inside presence, as memory. A 10-year-old girl's role-playing response to the question of where a dead person goes emphasizes remembering in context of the good:

> I think that she goes in the ground and goes in a little pieces of the soil but the heart goes to the family and makes them think about the good times with the person who dies and finally they feel better and go out and just have a good time. And the person who dies stays in the other people so they don't forget her and always think of the good times. (9)

A character in children's literature, Sammy (in *Thank You, Jackie Robinson*), also comes to believe in an immortality of memory; his dead friend Davy will always be seen in his mind's eye. Although Sammy is speaking of Jackie Robinson, the reader knows Sammy's words apply to Davy and that Sammy has made peace with the death: "In my mind, where nothing ever dies, I can see him still, to this very day, running from base to base in the top of the seventh inning, between the second and third out, in a brand-new baseball game that will never, ever be over" (7, pp. 124–125).

A more generalized presence is experienced as a diffuse bond of good feeling. In a Christian funeral service (in *The Magic Moth*), Maryanne's body is commended to the earth from whence it came and her spirit to heaven, a place of light, "more like the kind you feel inside when you love someone, like Maryanne" (4, p. 46). This consolation and the sense of continued connection are remarkably akin to the words of the poet Dylan Thomas: "Though lovers be lost, love shall not/And death shall have no dominion" (14, p. 77).

Death Arouses Anger, Diffuse and Unlimited

How should one behave when confronted with death? And how do those behaviors reflect feelings and judgments about the event and about oneself? Not eating, not playing, not enjoying oneself are ways of expressing mourning.

In *Thank You, Jackie Robinson,* young Sammy lost his most adult friend, his father-surrogate, Davy. After Davy's funeral, Sammy shuts himself in his room, determined to just sit there feeling sorry for himself. He refuses to turn on the radio and angrily rejects his mother's suggestion that he listen to the ball game, that special activity once shared between Davy and Sammy: "Who did she think she was, interfering with my misery?" (7, p. 121). Sammy is further angered because she does not tell him some story about Davy's soul being in heaven: "She didn't know for sure one way or the other. She could have fibbed a little to make me feel better and maybe I could have believed her fib for a little while" (7, p. 121).

But Sammy is also angry at his friend. Sammy blames Davy for his empty and lonely feelings. After all, if he had not known and loved this man Davy, his death would not make any difference. "'Tis better to have loved and lost than never loved at all" would, at this moment, be empty rhetoric. The reader is privy to Sammy's reasoning: "I would be just the way I had been before I'd known him. I'd be better of than I was, because right then I thought the hole in my stomach was going to last the rest of my life" (7, p. 117).

Six-year-old Mark-O (in *The Magic Moth*) is angry at everyone. He expresses his rage by locking himself in his room and refusing lunch. Mark-O's frustration at disrupted life and his fury at the visitors talking, laughing, and making noise is voiced to his mother: "I can't play the record player, and I can't get out the game box and I can't beat my drums and I can't. . . . Anyway, they shouldn't be laughing when Maryanne is dead" (4, p. 47).

Strong reaction against the usual activities of living (talking, eating, listening to the radio, playing) are not just acts of protest; they may also be expressions of blame and self-punishment. In *A Taste of Blackberries,* the child-narrator interprets talking, eating, even moving as "just like things were the same" as being somehow disloyal. He will do penance by nonparticipation and by fasting. Finally, after the funeral, when he allows himself to eat, he is surprised at how good everything tastes and at how ravishingly hungry he is. When his father reassures him, giving permission even to wolf down the food, this youngster, aware that his father has read his mind, tries to stifle his smile: " 'It's okay to smile too,' my dad said. 'Jamie would want you to do both.' Well, that sure was the truth. Jamie would be the last one to want me to go around sad and starving. I ate three servings of everything" (13, p. 67).

Anger may be understood as the underpinning for guilty judgments about one's feelings. In *By the Highway Home,* a while after news of her brother's death in Vietnam, 13-year-old Catty feels guilty for wanting life to resume some normalcy and good feelings. After criticizing her parents for the unrelenting atmosphere of somberness at home, she exposes her shame: " 'I want to pretend he's gone around the corner for an hour and forget him sometimes'—She pulled out of her mother's arms and leaned her head back closing her eyes. 'I'm not nice, am I?' she said slowly" (15, p. 25).

Death lingers in sadness, apparent and repressed. Good and bad qualities of the deceased plague the thoughts of survivors. A way to facilitate the mourning process is to encourage review of the relationship, however painful. In *Blew and the Death of the Mag,* Blew senses the pressure from people to cover her feelings and pretend everything is fine. In her innocence, she is aware of being preoccupied with *both* painful and happy memories. She wants to remember, show, and share her feelings, not only by laughing at happy thoughts, but by *crying at awful thoughts* (16, p. 57). In *The Tenth Best Thing about Barney,* a youngster is encouraged to recall *good* memories (10 of them) of his dead cat (17, p. 24). Caveat: repressing anger and memories, especially negative, uncomfortable reminiscences, lest the exposure and relieving be too painful, inhibits grieving.

Death Is Stigma and Embarrassment

Death is not easily tolerable, for it can breed shame. Recently, a college student confessed in a class to his sense of diminishment with regard to his father's death. He reported through his journal:

> Something you said in class the other day *really* hit home. You said you were surprised to hear that a child might (did) lie about her parents being alive. I used to lie all the time. When a teacher would ask up to junior high school age, what does your father do for a living, I would rarely say he is deceased. I always hated the word. Many times I would simply say he owns a candy store. (He did when he was alive.) I felt ashamed and embarrassed because I was different from everyone else. If I said he was dead, they would all feel sorry for me. I couldn't stand that and would rather lie. (9)

In *A Grief Observed,* the bereaved husband is acutely aware of others. The author, C. S. Lewis, shares the awareness that his loss is a source of embarrassment to those he meets. It seems a situation with no possible positive solution. In such a state, no behavior of others with regard to the loss, be it acknowledgment or denial, is acceptable to the bereaved: "At work, at the club, in the street, I see people, as they approach me, trying to make up their minds whether they'll say something about 'it' or not. I hate it if they do and if they don't" (18, p. 10).

Death as Punishment

A fourth-grade youngster is frightened and terrified by the prospect of death. His misconduct, elevated almost to a level of sinfulness, resulted in a desperate contact with a just and terrible God. Scrawled on a paper towel was his note, which read: "Dear God Please I don't want to die. I'll stop teasing and temper" (9).

Western-world youngsters coming from strong Christian and Puritan backgrounds, are familiar with tales and stories that conclude with the moral that death is punishment for sins or behaviors. Grünewald's painting, *The Damnation of Lovers* (19), is a horrendously graphic and frightful depiction of animals devouring the very portions of the flesh so enjoyed by the lustful lovers. *Struwwelpeter* is filled with such tales as "The Dreadful Story of Harriet and the Matches" and "The Story of Augustus Who Would not Eat His Soup." The fates of both child protagonists, conveyed in painstaking detail (though charmingly) in verse and image, are most extreme. Harriet is burned to death

> *... with all her clothes,*
> *And arms, and hands, and eyes, and nose;*
> *Till she had nothing more to lose*
> *Except her little scarlet shoes;*
> *And nothing else but these was found*
> *Among her ashes on the ground. (20, pp. 6–7)*

Robust Augustus, who refused to eat his soup, is sketched getting skinnier and skinnier until he completely disappears.

> *Look at him, now the fourth day's come*
> *He scarcely weighs a sugar-plum;*
> *He's like a little bit of thread,*
> *And on the fifth day, he was—dead! (20, p. 17)*

The final illustration is of his gravestone, marked by a cross and soup tureen.

Death is fraught with implications of responsibility. Bad thoughts or words can eventuate in someone's death, holding the living in uneasy bondage. In Vogel's story *My Twin Sister, Erika,* the surviving twin tries to forget she had once told her sister in a fit of anger that she wished her dead. She even tries to make herself believe that she never actually said the words. As her grandmother often told her, prayers and good thoughts have great power. Would not the reverse be also true? She wonders: "Was it possible bad thoughts had great power, too? Was it possible I had caused Erika's death?" (21, p. 52). Blew, too (in *Death of the Mag*), agonizes over her responsibility for her imaginary companion's illness and death. She starts playing games with herself. Her guilty thoughts ("if only") become promises and bargains:

> *If only I hadn't ever yelled at her, maybe she wouldn't have gotten sick....*
> *If only she gets better, I'll never hurt anybody ever....*
> *If only she gets well, I'll become a doctor, and never let anyone die....*
> *If only she lives, I'll never do anything wrong again.... (16, p. 33)*

Such reasoning, again, is not peculiar to children. In Kudret "Feast of the Dead," when Gulnaz hears the news of her husband's accidental death, she freezes, asking herself if this event is the punishment for her little tricks and her cheating. Her rationalizations to herself are clearly not convincing: "No, oh no, God could not be that cruel. This could not be anything but an accident. There were witnesses: he slipped, fell down, and died. Anybody could fall this way and die" (22, p. 162).

Death Is Controlling, Punishing

In turn, death can be punishment and the agency of revenge. Controlling others by the threat of suicide appears in film, song, and painting. Scene after scene in *Harold and Maude* (23) presents an adolescent son surprising his mother by suiciding in the bathtub, closet, anywhere to get her attention. In Elton John's popular favorite of the 1970s, "Suicide Rag," a teenager is taken with the idea of the scandal he would cause by shocking everyone with suicide. He fantasizes himself making the headline news. In the next-to-last stanza, the motivation for these thoughts becomes apparent:

> *A rift in my family,*
> *I can't use the car*
> *I gotta be in by 10 o'clock*
> *Who do they think they are? (24)*

Feeling impotent and angry at his parents' restrictions leads to a series of fantasies of acts that would cause them shame and remorse.

A 10-year-old expresses the power he has by the gesture of suicide. "They'll be sorry" is also the theme of Fig. 2. Just in time, the parent apologizes and thus aborts the event. In another drawing (Fig. 3), the suicide is successfully avoided by the (caring) parents' chastisement and punishment. Any concern, apology, or attention including that of anger, even hate, is welcome. Only indifference is unacceptable.

Young lovers, too, manipulate with the rescue fantasy. In Gilbert and Sullivan's marvelous parody "Tit-Willow," Ko-Ko wins Katisha with his tale of a poor bird downing himself in the name of unrequited love. Lest one missed Ko-Ko's intent in the

FIGURE 2

FIGURE 3

telling of such a maudlin story, the focus is switched from the bird to that of Katisha and quite clearly spelled out:

> And if you remain callous and obdurate, I
> Shall perish as he did, and you will know why,
> Though I probably shall not exclaim as I die,
> "O Willow titwillow, titwillow!" (25)

Roy Lichtenstein's *Drowning Girl* presents the same threat in painting. About to be engulfed by waves, a young woman, eyes brimming with tears, righteously, makes her thoughts known. Cartoon fashion, the blurb reads: "I'd rather sink than call Brad for help" (26).

A sequence drawing by a youngster (Fig. 4) dramatizes again the vengeful anger inherent in a suicide threat wherein the explanation that "they'll be sorry" is made explicit. Once again, one's personal death, an extraordinary price in terms of self-punishment, is envisioned as an instrument of controlling others.

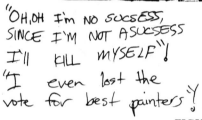

FIGURE 4

Contagion of Death

Can one "catch" dying? Is the idea of death too much to bear close witness? Both Figures 5 and 6 suggest resistance and fear on the part of the visitor to the dying. In a 16-year-old boy's drawing (Fig. 5), the son wants to talk to his mother from a distance. One might speculate that not coming closer for this final conversation, or the cavalier attitude on his part, allows for denial of sorts: If the last words are not spoken, the death cannot yet happen. But the boy's response—words, stance, and distance—suggest fear of contamination or contagion.

In a 12-year-old's drawing (Fig. 6), the young visitor's thoughts are made explicit through the caption. He sees himself in the casket at his own funeral if he shares the soda offered by his friend with leukemia. Both these drawings expose another truth: Visiting the dying is exposure to the sadness of the

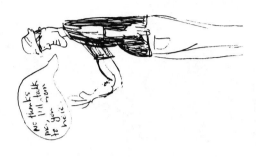

FIGURE 5

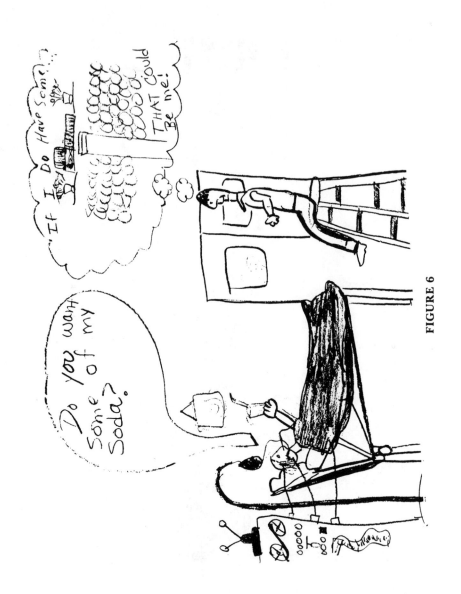

FIGURE 6

situation. One will be tainted by grief, feelings of self-pity, and sorrow as one bears the loneliness of the eventual separation.

Thinking about the dead is painful. In an unpublished manuscript, young Dusty is able only to think about his dead friend a little at a time. Sometimes his sadness is so great he feels his stomach hurting. As he tries to make sense of his friend's accidental death, the progression of thoughts leads directly to those concerning his own future: "I don't see why Dusty had to die. . . . I don't want to die. I want to get to be a grown-up so I'm taller than my Dad and I can be a deep sea diver or a veterinarian and stay up late" (27).

In the Gerard Manley Hopkins poem "Spring and Fall to a Young Child," the scenario is an inocuous situation. A youngster, Margaret, muses on the dying leaves of autumn, on "goldengrove unleaving." Her sigh is the realization all living things must die, and in the final couplet, she makes the association to her own inevitable death: "It is the blight man was born for/It is Margaret you mourn for" (28, p. 89). As no man is an island (29), no witness to dying can remain insular, invulnerable to sadness, distress, or confrontation with thoughts of his or her own mortality. One is touched by being in contact with death.

Murderous Impulses

If we are "afraid" of death's visage, what better way of mastering the fear than aligning oneself with the power of death-giving. But the murderous impulse is not readily borne without self-judgment.

"The Day of the Robin" (9) is a short story recalling the incident of stoning a bird to death. Skipping school with a friend, two fourth graders happen upon a bird with a broken wing, fluttering feebly, still trying to fly: "I have forgotten whose idea it was first. I hope it was Oliver's. We decided the robin must be put out of it's misery; it must be killed." The actual execution, ironically precipitated by the boy's memory of a picture of St. Stephen, was to be carried out with a stone. But the bird did not die as instantly as anticipated: "Then we grew

frightened . . . and we took more stones and threw them as hard
as we could at the robin. . . . The stones fell one upon the other
until the bird was covered except for its head . . . and still it
was not dead." After a final smash, the boys stand silently for a
long time, physically separated by the pile of stones between
them, unable even to face one another. Their shame and regret
erupts in tears: "No sound but the distant shouts of our
classmates playing on the lawn. The sun shone brilliantly:
nothing had changed in the world, but without a word and at
the same moment, we both began to cry."

In Steinbeck's novel *The Red Pony,* little Jody, motivated
by boredom, baits a rat trap with stale cheese, intending to set
it where a dog would get his nose snapped. Another time, Jody
kills and dismembers a bird. As in "The Day of the Robin," the
guilt, shame, and remorse occur after the frenzy of the activity.
Jody did not care what older people would say if they had seen
him kill the bird; but in retrospect, he was ashamed because of
their potential opinion: "He decided to forget the whole thing
as quickly as he could, and never to mention it (30, p. 63).

Feelings of aggression find expression in daring adventure.
Such a bold act transformed the boys in "The Day of the
Robin." Crying together was not the only outlet for the boys
who stoned the bird; the author was able to "mention" the deed
by the very act of writing the story. Not so for Jody, who has
no chance to share his guilty secret. No confessional. No chance
to do penance or transcend his shame. Jody is saddled with the
added burden of repressing his uncomfortable feelings.

Traditionally, societies have provided outlets for such
impulses and fantasies through the grimmest of horror stories and
fairy tales. An African lullaby, "Simba-Ba," or "Mama's Baby,"
translates: "Twist his neck and hit him on the head/Throw him
in the ditch and he'll be dead." Similarly, the Western lullaby
"Rock-a-bye-baby" outlines an unhappy accident. Sleeping
peacefully in a cradle fastened high in a tree, a baby falls when a
bough breaks. Motifs not only of unhappy endings but of
cruelty are evident:

> There was a little man, and he had a little gun
> And his bullets were made of lead, lead, lead.

And he went to the brook and shot a little duck
Right in the middle of the head, head, head.

Clarence Darrow's confession that he never wanted to see anybody die but that there were a few obituary notices he has read with pleasure helps us feel less lonely with our fantasies of having wished certain people dead. Gilbert and Sullivan's Lord High Executioner receives much applause and knowing chuckles as he enumerates in great detail his little list of those who never would be missed (31). Children sing with gusto of their one and only counselor who died committing suicide; "She did it just to spite us/It really did delight us." The limericks and aphorisms were intended neither to frighten nor to evoke feelings of sorrow, guilt, or remorse. Quite the contrary. Humor, irony, and such gestures of scorn as sick humor allow for release, albeit temporary, of pent-up anxieties.

Murderous impulses can be safely embedded in fiction, fairy tales, and drama. Being human, by definition, admits to behaviors other than the saintly. But merely naming the devil, as in the tale of Rumplestiltskin—just acknowledging one's destructive impulses—is not enough. One must face again and again their unsettling existence. In *After the Fall*, Arthur Miller, goes further than acceptance. The knowing is not all: "The wish to kill is never killed, but with some gift of courage one may look into its face when it appears, and with a stroke of love—as to an idiot in the house—forgive it; again and again . . . forever" (32, p. 128).

Conclusion

Children and others seem to view death in multiple ways. Death happens to people, and the event itself arouses concerns for ongoing living of the survivors as well as for ongoing living of the deceased. Children's images seem fancifully occupied with where the dead go; but adults, too, seem anxious to transmit their own convictions of the place of residence of the deceased. For all, death arouses need for connectedness and continuation of relationship.

Death is also an instrument of feelings. Shame, remorse, guilt, and anger, though common enough emotions, can be overwhelming. Literature and the arts help make such anguish bearable. The arts, reflecting life, are arenas where contradictions can coexist, where neither the bright nor the dark must eradicate the other's existence. They provide a sense of comfort and kinship as they give voice to the unmentionable and most inner torments.

Death gives one power. Again, the art forms, story and painting, provide insight into how children and others use a death threat for revenge, for control of others, and for punishment of actions that are not acceptable.

Thus death in its actual and symbolic manifestations presents a panoply of human concerns and expressions that appear quite early in life. The child's concerns are society's concerns. A society's art forms lend to these concerns focus, explanation, ritual, and legitimacy. As a vehicle for expression, they allow us to prevail over pain, to transcend and partly end it by transforming it into "art."

References

1. Anthony, S. *The child's discovery of death.* New York: Harcourt, 1940.
2. Nagy, M. The child's view of death. In H. Feifel (Ed.), *The meaning of death.* New York: McGraw-Hill, 1959, pp. 79–98.
3. Coburn, J. *Anne and the sand dobbies.* New York: Seabury, 1964.
4. Lee, V. *The magic moth,* New York: Seabury, 1972.
5. Allen, W. *New Yorker,* January 20, 1973, pp. 32–33.
6. Dickinson, E. I never saw a moor. In Williams & Honige (Eds.), *The mentor book of major American poets.* New York: New American Library, 1962.
7. Cohen, B. *Thank you, Jackie Robinson.* New York: Lothrop, 1974.
8. Adler, B. You don't have to do homework in heaven. *Good Housekeeping,* March 1979, p. 46.
9. Bertman, S. *Death education, a primer for all ages.* Unpublished manuscript, Equinox Institute, Boston, Mass.
10. Lee, M. *The rock and the willow.* New York: Lothrop, 1963.
11. Gauguin, P. The spirit of the dead watching. In C. Estienne, *Gauguin.* Cleveland: Skira, 1953. (Painting)
12. Alcott, L. *Little women.* Boston: Little, Brown, 1968.

13. Smith, D. *A taste of blackberries.* New York: Crowell, 1973.
14. Thomas, D. And death shall have no dominion. *Collected poems of Dylan Thomas.* New York: New Directions, 1939.
15. Stolz, M. *By the highway home.* New York: Harper, 1971.
16. Lichtman, W. *Blew and the death of the mag.* Albion, Freestone, 1975.
17. Viorst, J. *The tenth good thing about Barney.* New York: Atheneum, 1971.
18. Lewis, C. S. *A grief observed.* New York: Seabury, 1963.
19. Grünewald, M. *Damnation of lovers.* Strasbourg: Cathedral Museum, 15th century. (Painting)
20. Hoffman, H. *Struwwelpeter.* New York: Warne, 1944.
21. Vogel, I. *My twin sister, Erika.* New York: Harper, 1976.
22. Kudret, C. Feast of the dead. In Adler & Stanford (Eds.), *We are but a moments sunlight.* New York: Pocket Books, 1976.
23. *Harold and Maude.* Los Angeles: Paramount, 1971. (Film)
24. John, E., *Honky chateau* "Think I'm gonna kill myself, suicide rag." Universal City: MCA, 1972. (Music)
25. Gilbert, W., & Sullivan, A. Willow, tit-willow. In *The Mikado.* London: Chappell, 1911, pp. 208-212. (Music)
26. Lichtenstein, R. *Drowning girl.* New York: Museum of Modern Art, 1970. (Painting)
27. Clardy, A. *Dusty was my friend.* Unpublished manuscript.
28. Hopkins, G. Spring and fall to a young child. Gardner & MacKenzie, (Eds.), *Poems of G. M. Hopkins.* New York: Oxford University Press, 1967, pp. 88-89.
29. Donne, J. Devotions. *The complete poetry and selected prose of John Donne and the complete poetry of William Blake.* New York: Random House, 1941.
30. Steinbeck, J. *The red pony.* New York: Viking, 1959.
31. Gilbert, W., & Sullivan, A. Lord High Executioner, In *The Mikado.* London: Chappell, 1911, pp. 267-270.
32. Miller, A. *After the Fall.* New York: Viking, 1964.

Request reprints from Sandra L. Bertman, Humanities in Medicine, University of Massachusetts Medical School, Worcester, MA.

THE PASTORAL COUNSELOR AND THE CHILD
ENCOUNTERING DEATH

EDGAR N. JACKSON

The world of the child is special. When people become adult, they seem to lose touch with the child who lurks within each of them as well as with the child each once was. This makes it difficult to understand children and communicate effectively with them. Young children live in a world where feelings supply most of the life experiences. It is a world that can be both lyrical and frightening, rich in poetic imagery and yet stark in its frightening realities. Trivial events can add delirious joy and excitement to life; yet comparable events can produce painful feelings of fear and abandonment.

It is in this context of a children's world that we have to explore the meaning of their encounters with death. It is a wonderful world of imagination where perceptions tend to create a different brand of reality (1). It is adventurous in the games that are played, where monsters are created at will, and where wonder comes alive in events that may be commonplace for those who have lived a little longer. A child may be defensive but seldom blasé. The child's world has boundaries that are drawn in closely and tightly. What is the impact on this small world of a large experience like the confronting of death? One does not ask this question apart from an interpretation of the powerful emotional drives of young children. Grief and loss stimulate painful emotions in the child, for they are aimed at the security system that is rooted in utter dependence on others (2). Feelings of abandonment are related to fears of death, for the young child cannot make it on his own (3).

This dependence is interrelated with the total emotional life of the child. The child is capable of great grief, but the source of grief may be quite different from that of an adult. The adult knows space and time; the young child does not. Space and time are essential to a concept of death. So the young child obviously experiences acute grief without any concept of death. This may lead adults to fail to understand the intensity of the child's grief. Young children do not fear the death of others, for they cannot conceive it (1, 4–5). Their grief is bound up with their complete dependence for life support and with the fear of the loss of their security. With young children, even the people in their environment are secondary to their security. At early ages they are able to transfer the focus of feelings from one person to another without apparent trauma. Someone to play with, pay attention to, and communicate with a child as well as to meet physical and emotional needs becomes a surrogate who may fill the security needs in place of a parent. But what would be true in this regard for a two-year-old would not be the case for a four-year-old.

So, with young children, emotions are powerfully affected by feelings of insecurity that may be only tangentially related to space, time, and people. Death is not apt to be a part of the reality structure of a young child, but feelings related to separation, abandonment, fear of rejection, and apprehension about threats to security such as loud and violent sounding voices can be as traumatic as feelings about death would be for older children and adults.

The world of the child is unique because of the feelings with which the child furnishes that world. The feelings are so completely integrated into the life structure of the child that they cannot easily be isolated for study. Even the efforts of Jean Piaget, extensive and imaginative as they are, tend to be largely descriptive rather than philosophical in their end results.

LeBoyer (6) provides a meaningful interpretation of the initial stages of human attachment through his description of how the skin becomes the starting point for intense human interaction. Starting prenatally with the skin massage by the amniotic fluid, the body covering is sensitized by this process of gentling. At its best, in the absence of acute spasticity, the passage through the birth canal adds to the message process. Immediately after birth, the varied sensations of the prenatal state continue by placing the infant on the breast, where the rhythms of the heart, the warmth of the skin, and gentle massage can approximate the prenatal sensations. Wisely instituted, this procedure can become the basis for trust and positive organic responses to life outside the privileged climate of the uterus.

Instead of the positive experience of the type LeBoyer encourages, birth may have the opposite results when the newborn is whisked away and placed in a nursery with its unfamiliar bustle, harsh lights, strange noises, and the generalized feelings of separation and abandonment. The neonatal organism may be started in the direction of feeling rejected and distrusting those around. It may further be moved in the direction of active efforts at self-protection by the use of alternatives to love, the overt expressions of hostility that may show up in organic or inorganic behavior. Here we may have the starting point for the sickly, disturbed, or hostile child in the infant who uses the best alternatives available to gain some security and support in an outside world that appears to be largely unconcerned with the interests of the neonate.

Applying Knowledge of the Child's Development

Pastors or other counselors can probably measure their effectiveness by their degree of understanding of the developmental process that defines the emotional growth of the child. With the young child what one does is far more important than what one says. The young child experiences death as abandonment, and so the therapeutic intervention should be directed toward dispelling those feelings. How would that be done? Usually it is best done by applying large doses of tender love and care. This involves holding the child, cuddling and stroking the skin. Any talking should center on the timbre or emotional quality of the sounds, with soft and soothing sounds producing a gentling effect in as many dimensions of sensory response as possible. While it is important to understand where the child is in emotional development, it is even more important to do the things that the child can immediately integrate into basic emotional needs.

If we understand the term *young child* to be those aged from birth to about three, the next stage in development would come from about four to seven years. Here the elements of infancy are past and we have a human being who is using language to supplement a whole variety of other methods of exploration. Children at this age are apt to be curious, quite literal, and actively engaged in exploring verbally and otherwise. Although grouping children by age can be helpful in understanding the general characteristics of a child, it is always wise to keep in mind that each child is unique. Children differ in their rates of development, and they are shaped by the experiences of their lives (3, p. 58-59).

Adults often fail to realize how much they modify language by common usage. Children have not usually developed these refinements and so may show their confusion. If in response to the child's question, "Where has grandpa gone?" an effort is made to speak of a state of pure spirit sometimes referred to as heaven, the child is apt to question further: "Then why did they put his body in a hole in the groud?" When asked if she would like to go to the funeral home to see her grandmother's body for the last time, a young girl responded, "No, I don't want to see Grandma with her head cut off." In her literal use of language, a "body" was that portion of the anatomy from the neck down.

Children during this stage are not only literal but quite body oriented. They are interested in the physical functions and characteristics of their own bodies and the bodies of other people as well. The questions they ask about death are apt to be oriented to this body interest. They may ask questions such as How do you eat when you are dead? or How do you go to the bathroom when you are dead? For them, such questions are completely logical, for they are trying to discover the difference between being dead and alive. For them, it is difficult to know what is lost in the process of dying.

It becomes quite clear for the counselor, then, that the use of abstract language in responding to such direct seeking for information would be self-defeating and possibly damaging. To talk about "going to be with Jesus" may well sound like an evasion to the child. The child needs simple and accurate answers to frame the developing concept of death and its meaning.

I mentioned the damaging answer. Though often given with good intentions, a child's perspective may be so literal that, in acting on it, injury may occur. A four-year-old was brought to a child guidance clinic because of what appeared to be repeated suicidal acts. Exploration of the behavior showed it was quite logical to the child. Her dog had been killed by a car. She was told that her puppy had gone to dog heaven and that if she would be a good girl she would go there too. From the perspective of her grief, the logical answer was to run in front of a car. Several drivers suffered traumatic experiences in trying to avoid hitting the child. How much better it would have been for everyone if the parents had used the child's encounter with death as an educational opportunity. They could as easily have said, "What a sad thing that your puppy had not learned to stay out of the road. I hope this teaches you never to run out into the road without first making sure that there are no cars coming from either direction."

Every death experience for a child can be a learning opportunity. Death is so much a part of the life of a child that it is imperative that it be dealt with in positive ways. Death is the central event of many holidays, for instance, the turkey at Thanksgiving, the hamburger at the picnic, and the fish fry after the day at the brook. If death can be interpreted as a contribution to life, a more positive perspective can be maintained, and the grief can then be understood for what it is—a personal loss. Not all death is bad. It is the death we have difficulty coping with that is painful. So we do not wisely rail against death. Rather, we learn to develop skills in managing the distress that comes with acute personal loss. These skills can begin to develop early in life with proper guidance.

The Pastoral Counselor's Role

The pastor needs to be especially on guard against the unwise use of complex abstractions with younger children. In talking with a young child, it is usually fruitful to listen and ask

open-ended questions until it is quite clear what the child is
thinking and feeling. Otherwise there may be wasted answers to
questions that do not exist. Sometimes the questions a child
asks may entrap the person who fails to understand where the
line of questioning is going.

Let us take two lines of questioning. The minister is visiting
a sick relative, and seven-year-old Johnny asks the pastor, "Can
God do anything?" The pastor, who feels called upon to defend
God, responds, "Oh, yes, God is all powerful; God can do
anything if he wants to." Johnny responds, "I'm glad. Then God
can keep my uncle from dying. He's my favorite uncle. We do
lots of things together." When the uncle dies, Johnny is left
with a dilemma. Either God did not want to save the uncle or
really did not care and let Johnny down, or God was not as
powerful as he was supposed to be.

There could be another and more useful response to the
same question, "Can God do anything?" The pastor could use
an open-ended question to find out more of what Johnny wants
to know. She or he could say, "Tell me, Johnny, just how do
you mean that?" "Well, Uncle Paul is very sick. He might die. I
don't want him to die. Could God keep him from dying?" The
pastor responds, "I see what you mean. God has great power. It
shows all about us in creation. When God made the universe it
could only be held together by the laws of creation. Our bodies
have laws also. If you fall off the roof, you could be hurt. If
you violate the laws of health you can be hurt. The power of
God is shown through the laws of the universe he has created.
So you would not expect God to violate his own laws, would
you?" This line of response would be developed to make
Johnny responsible for his own health and welfare. It would
affirm the power of God without expecting God to violate his
own nature. It would make it easier at some future time for
Johnny to learn to cooperate with God's laws rather than violate
them. As an authority figure with important teaching functions,
the pastor can be important as a helper for children who are
trying to learn how to cope with both life and death.

When children become a bit older—8 to 11—their perspectives change. Time and space are more clearly defined, for them
and the people who are a part of their lives are more numerous.

Interests change, and this affects their perceptions of death. Instead of a physical interest in death there develops a social concern about death and its implications for life. Because the interrelations of life have become more significant, the impact of death on human relations tends to become more important (4).

This change in relation will show itself in behavior, verbal and otherwise. Instead of curiosity about the physical qualities of death, there will be a more active concern about what happens to people who encounter death. The growing edge of awareness will show itself in the questions asked. The child will be more apt to inquire about what happens to the social fabric of life when death is encountered: "Who will take care of the Johnson children now?" or "Will Jane and Ted have to move away now that their father is dead?"

In contrast to the four- to seven-year-old with a primary interest in the physical meaning of death, the responses will be quite different. Where the four- to seven-year-old needs simple and direct answers to simple questions of information, the more socially interested youngster needs reassurance and an understanding of social processes. The 8- to 11-year-old is apt to bring his own concern about death into the picture. Some of his questions may be exploring the consequences of death for his own life.

The effort to make some sense out of death may show up in questions that may seem unacceptable. When a favorite grandfather died and a feeble great-grandmother lived on, an eight-year-old asked, "Why did Grandpa die and Great-grandma is still alive?" The logic of the question was clear for the eight-year-old even though the child was warned not to talk like that when the great-grandmother could hear. Everyone seemed embarrassed when the same child went to her grandmother and asked, "When are you going to die?" When trying to frame a socially acceptable idea of the relation of life and death, such questions are to be expected. The effort to make sense out of a baffling mystery should be encouraged because the sooner some sense is made, the better for those who will encounter the mystery repeatedly.

Underlying many questions emerging from this age group are security issues. A growing awareness of social dependency carries with it a concern for personal security. When a child asks, "Who will take care of Fred now that his parents were killed?" the implication quite clearly is "Who will take care of me if my parents are killed in an accident?" While it would be unwise to give glib and superficial reassurance, it is essential that the child have a clearer understanding of the broader fabric of family and community life. The reassurance should be honest but optimistic. Parents might say, "I see what you mean, but we expect to be around for a long time; and even if we might not be, there are other people who love you and would take care of you."

I remember an 11-year-old who was being treated at the psychiatric clinic for children that I headed. His father died quite rapidly of a virulent neoplastic involvement. The child had been building a sailboat with his father. When I visited the family, William was not present. When I asked about him, I was told he was out in the garage. So I went out and found him sitting glumly, looking at the unfinished sailboat. When we talked about his feelings it was obvious that he took the death very personally at the point of unfinished business, made specific by the incomplete sailboat. He resented his father's death and felt cheated. It was out of this set of feelings that we began to build a larger view of life and its vagaries. We worked out some plans for finishing the boat, for that was where he was encountering his grief most specifically. We ended our talk with the clarified idea that his father did not die on purpose to create a problem, but that some times in life we have to adjust our programs and plans. The important idea is to understand and adapt to change rather than feeling defeated and bitter. William went back into the house with me and joined the rest of the group.

When we consider the orientation and needs of the adolescent or preadolescent, we are moving into quite different territory. The skill in using language and other abstractions has been developed to the point at which it can be a useful resource. At the same time, the intensity of feelings makes it possible for grief to be a powerful force in life.

Let us look first at the preadolescent. The age boundaries here are not clearly set, for there are considerable variations in how psychophysical development takes place. But usually preadolescence means 11- to 13-year-olds, or those in the junior high level of education. Clinical experience makes it quite clear that this age is a time of recapitulation and consolidation of past experience. It seems that the experiences of the first years of life are restated in a different context. If there has been security and healthy development from birth to three, the years of infancy, there is apt to be a secure and untroubled movement into a larger social orientation of life. If, however, the early years have been fraught with uncertainty and conflict this is apt to be acted out in a larger circle of relationships with hostility and conflict with authority figures. This tends to lay the foundation for emerging ego development in maladaptive forms of social adjustment. Instead of testing the boundaries of social behavior to learn how to conform, there is apt to be an assault on the boundaries to act out hostility. May, in his book *The Meaning of Anxiety* (7), points out the relationship between antisocial behavior and the experience of death or its emotional equivalent early in life.

The preadolescent tends to act out deep feelings in behavior. If the feelings are satisfying, the behavior will tend to be pleasant, socially cooperative, and personally rewarding. If the feelings grow from frustration and resentment, the behavior may be hostile, destructive, and further injuring of the self-esteem, which is already damaged. The encounter with death may show up in extremes of behavior, from, on the one hand, actions unrelated to the event, to, on the other hand, overcompensation in acting out.

Therapeutic intervention will involve talking out the feelings fully, and the ability to talk about feelings may be fully realized at this age. Also, ceremonial acting out will be meaningful, for it usually combines large-muscle activity with conceptualization and abstract language. Much time may be spent in talking about the meaning of life and death with an intensely personal focus. Preadolescents may enter into this talk with difficulty, however, especially with adults. Here, the sharing of thoughts and feelings with a peer group would be more characteristic. This can be a time of emerging idealism, when the heroic and symbolic are enhanced by an active imagination.

The preadolescent is in a time of transition from the dependency of childhood to the more venturesome thinking and acting of adolescence. The combination of the dependent and the independent in thinking and feeling may thus be manifest in ways that, though they appear incongruous, are congruent with the age and state of personal development. Overidentification may show itself in forms of grief that are acted out toward popular figures like Elvis Presley, whose untimely death had a major impact on this age group.

The next stage, adolescence, brings preadolescent behavior to its fuller expression. In positive form it may be life commitment wherein teen-agers decide on the goals for life. Here the heroic may be a statement of faith in the value of life and a desire to make the most of it. A negative attitude toward life may be expressed in the symbolic self-destruction of drug use and the toying with life in such games as Russian roulette and playing chicken with automobiles, where life is risked in acts of bravado. Yet it seems that the underlying statement is one of fear and insecurity. It is as if the game players were saying, "I am not afraid of death, for I make a plaything out of it"; yet the real meaning of their negative behavior may be: "I am so afraid of death that I may be able to control my fear if I reduce my thinking of death to the level of game playing."

The pastoral counselor with teen-agers may find that the emotional commitment is strong and oriented toward the self. Adolescents are apt to think that they are the discoverers of deep and powerful feelings and that no one has ever loved as they love. As love is the other side of the coin of grief, they are highly vulnerable. Because at their stage of development they are self-centered, their love is primarily for themselves and their own feelings, however, and for others only in a secondary way. Thus, they can be doubly distressed. It is a time when they are trying to learn the complicated art of object love, and the learning process is as painful as it is experimental. Though they may shift the focus of love quickly from one person to another, the object tends to be the self. Being in love with love, as in the case of "puppy love," both the idealism and the focus on self enhance the grief when the relationship is broken. Emotional injury at this point may last a life time unless there is wise and skillful intervention. Self-destructive behavior is quite common as a mode of resolving grief among teen-agers.

Cheryl was 16 and attending the junior prom at the time her father died of a heart attack in a motel in a distant city. When she received the news of his death the next day, she was overwhelmed with guilt and grief. That she was having the most wonderful time of her life at the very time her father was dying a lonely death made her experience even more poignant. She locked herself in her room, would speak to no one, and at first ate no food. On the second day of her self-imposed imprisonment, she opened the door to take a tray left for her. On the day of the funeral she was still in her room. When the pastor was informed of her behavior, he came to the house and, through the door, identified himself. He said, "Cheryl, I want to talk with you." After a few moments of silence he heard the key turn in the lock, and he entered the room. He explained the function of the funeral as a tribute to a life that has been lived. He told Cheryl he assumed that she would want to use this opportunity to show her love for her father. She cried, and he accepted her feelings of guilt and grief. She said that no one could feel the way she did, and the pastor affirmed the uniqueness of each person's feelings. After an hour of deep sharing, Cheryl walked out of her room and was reunited with other members of her family. Her behavior was typical of the adolescent in its dramatic action, its self-centered attitude toward a life crisis, and its willingness to respond to an authority figure who was outside of the immediate family.

Pastors have some advantages as counselors because of their easy availability; their in-depth knowledge of families and family members, their strengths and weaknesses; and their ability to move toward people in crises—a privilege not usually granted to any other counselors.

The skills that pastors have acquired as counselors are fortified by the fact that they are able to add a cosmic dimension to the counseling process. They are not afraid to talk about the spiritual aspects of life and the value systems that make it possible for a person to develop inner strength essential to adequate coping skill. Pastors know the importance of attitudes and the place they play in inner stability. Some things are assumed in the pastor's role, so they do not even need to be talked about. Although this may at some point create hazards, it is usually a useful resource.

Counselors of children and the clergy especially have an opportunity to resolve problems that might otherwise plague life for decades. To be effective, they must look at the problem from the child's point of view. This means that they must be clear about the developmental stage of the child so that they are working effectively toward the child's real needs. Also it is important for them to have a working knowledge of the family and social structure within which the child lives and develops feelings. There must be a working knowledge of how others in the family respond to crises and what the emotional learning experience of the child has been.

Some Guidelines for Counseling Children

There are several more specific guidelines for counseling children in the home and family context. These might be shared with other adults so that counselors and family are not working at cross-purposes.

First, children have a right to expect honest answers to their questions. Gorer (8) points out in his study that many adults ignore the questions asked with the implication that the questions are improper or inappropriate. The rest admit that they give answers that they do not believe but cannot think of anything else to say. This is poor treatment of the growing edge of a child's interest in an important subject such as death. Children are so sensitive to emotional content in communication that the built-in lie detector immediately goes to work. Children may lose confidence in the adults to whom their queries are directed. They also are denied the basic information they need for developing a working understanding of life crises. Invariably they will go elsewhere for answers and often find those that are inadequate and threatening. The breakdown in communication also tends to be projected into the future with the feeling that, if there are important answers to be sought, they cannot be found with certain adults, who are obviously threatened.

Second, children have a right to be understood in their own stages of development. Adults tend to be preoccupied with their own thoughts and feelings. It is so important to sharpen up the communication by asking questions like "How do you mean? or Let me be sure I understand; could you be more specific? Then the communication will not break down.

Third, counselors should try to avoid communicating anxiety. When an adult overanswers or underanswers, the anxiety shows through. When a child is trying to grow in understanding, information is important, not disturbing emotion. If anxiety is pervasive the emotion may outweigh the information, and then the emotion may be carried along for a long time. The emotion attached to childhood events continue to plague many adults long after the original problem has been resolved. Children are largely defenseless against the strong emotions of the adults around them, so special care should be taken not to inundate a child. If some adults are disturbed, it then becomes important for other adults to step in and cope with the child's queries with well-balanced emotions.

Fourth, children benefit from large-muscle activity that is related to the crisis. Here the established forms of acting out are beneficial. A child does not have to understand all of the ramifications of a rite, ritual, or ceremony to participate at the level of emotional need. A little girl does not need to know all about human sexuality to be a flowergirl at a wedding. Nor does a child have to understand all about death to participate in a funeral. Ceremonies are made to order for children, for they can participate at their level of comprehension. Adults often err in trying to protect children from funerals. They tend to project their more adult understanding. As a general rule, a child should not be excluded from important family activities, and this would include funerals. If a child does not want to attend, it is already a sign that undue anxiety has been created, and that problem should be faced. If it is not, the anxiety could be cumulative, and the child could be denied the most effective and easily accessible therapeutic intervention that the community provides. Yet children should never be forced to attend or to do things that cause them discomfort. If left alone to do their own exploring, they will find answers to their questions within the range of their own thoughts and feelings.

Fifth, counselors need to remember that children have the capacity for stronger feelings of separation and abandonment than from an understanding of the meaning of death. The growing edge of the child's consciousness is constantly providing opportunities for exploring the nature and qualities of the death experience. It is possible to build a discriminating attitude that knows there are different forms of death. This discrimination makes it possible to enjoy a turkey at Thanksgiving without feeling guilt and at the same time to learn to protect life and health by wise avoidance of the things that could injure life.

Sixth, counselors should remember that every death encounter is an educational opportunity. Wisely managed, it can provide the long-term security to life. Unwisely managed, it can project anxiety and unwise behavior into the future so that it cumulatively impairs life. Pastoral counselors, through counseling, ceremonial activity, and an educational program, are able to provide resources for growth into a mature and discriminative attitude toward life and death.

Conclusion

In times of crisis when emotions run strong, the wise counselor who knows the family and its relationships but is not bound up with its emotions can be a primary therapeutic resource. With children, the counseling opportunity is especially advantageous, for if the early experiences can be handled well, a pattern is set for the wise management of ensuing life events.

The special needs and special opportunities related to counseling children warrant careful study. The methods and the techniques are so different that they are learned only by special efforts. But the benefits in the lives of the children served may well add blessings to life for a whole lifetime.

References

1. Piaget, J. *The child's conception of the world* (C. K. Ogden, Ed.). Totowa, N.J.: Littlefield, Adams, 1965.
2. Bowlby, J. Separation anxiety. *International Journal of Psychoanalysis,* 1960, *41,* 89–113.

3. Rochlin, G. The dread of abandonment: A contribution to the etiology of the loss complex and to depression. In *The psychoanalytic study of the child.* New York: International Universities, 1961, *16*, 451–470.
4. Jackson, E. *Telling a child about death.* New York: Hawthorn, 1965.
5. Jackson, E. *The many faces of grief.* Nashville: Abingdon, 1972.
6. LeBoyer, F. *Birth without violence.* New York: Knopf, 1976.
7. May, R. *The meaning of anxiety.* New York: Ronald, 1950.
8. Gorer, G. *Death, Grief and Mourning.* New York Doubleday, 1965.

Request reprints from Edgar N. Jackson, Washington Road, Corinth, Vermont 05039.

HELPING WITH DEATH EDUCATION

CHARLES A. CORR

An effective educational program must in part attempt to correct imbalances in our individual and social perceptions of death. Some counterbalances to these perceptions that weigh on the side of a new and more desirable equilibrium are relevant to the aims of this chapter. In the first place, I do not set out here to create new specialists. True expertise is not to be slighted. But my goal is in the main to provide guidelines for ordinary folk who want to be more helpful to children. Second, because education about death and dying in the best sense is properly education about life and living, I am really assisting people to recapture and implement perspectives on life that for many have somehow gone slightly out of focus. Third, this achievement is not beyond the capacities of most people. In general, they will need an opportunity and some direction for examining their own perceptions of death, a certain amount of information, an appreciation of typical concerns of children, a chance to benefit from the viewpoints of others, and practice in elementary interactions skills. Many people with a little time, energy, motivation, and some resources may be able to prepare themselves for this work. Most will benefit from a bit more organized or formal assistance.

The principal divisions of this chapter explore guidelines, preparation, and resources for helping with death education. The first of these subdivisions considers opportunities, responsibilities, and goals for death education with children; the second looks at formal and informal contexts in which to prepare helpers; and the third outlines different types of resources that are available for use by helpers. In addition to its relevance here, this last part of the chapter also lays a foundation for the section, "Resources," which offers annotated descriptions of books for adults and for children, and of audiovisual resources that might be used in helping children. I close with a short caution about what is, or should be, involved in efforts at helping the helpers.

Guidelines for Helping

Opportunities

Just as death is a natural part of life, opportunities for education about death arise in the midst of living. They can be of many sorts. Some are planned, formal courses of instruction, but often the most significant are unanticipated, informal occasions that might arise from an encounter with a dead animal on a hike, a timid question that seems suddenly to come from nowhere, or the sharing of a child's anxieties at bedtime. Some of these opportunities center on a request for information; others seek emotional support; and still others require no more than a chance for the child to express a concern or explore an idea. For adults, "death education" is a phrase with many ramifications, encompassing what we understand as didactic teaching as well as guiding of experiences, discussion of ideas, offering of sympathy, and inculcation of values. Because death education has such broad significance and its occasions are so widespread, few adults can expect to avoid it altogether. Here four of the most common types of opportunities for death education are identified as a way of sensitizing readers to possibilities and widening the scope of their vision in at least a preliminary way.

When the phrase "death education" is first mentioned, perhaps the most likely model to come to mind is a formal course on death and dying. Such courses are now widespread in North American high schools, colleges, and universities (1). The very rapidity of their proliferation since the publication in 1959 of Feifel's pioneering text *The Meaning of Death* (2), and especially during the 1970s, demonstrates the great interest that there is in this subject, particularly within the upper years of our educational system. Courses of this sort are sometimes taught by a single instructor or from the standpoint of a particular profession or academic discipline. They may have greater richness, however, when conceived as interdisciplinary experiences or when team-taught by people from complementary backgrounds. The diversity of such courses may bewilder those who approach this field for the first time. Nevertheless, a substantial body of literature that describes such courses has become available, and annotated descriptions of that literature in a recent resource guide (3) have greatly facilitated access. Also helpful are an outline of a model syllabus for a comprehensive death and dying course at the college level (4) and discussion of goals and strategies for death education (5-7).

Another manifestation of death education within standard academic settings has occurred in the form of units or aspects of other courses offered within traditional disciplines or subject areas. Thus, one might find a unit on death and dying within a health education course; discussion of biologic aspects of death in a science curriculum; exploration of funeral costs as an example of economic and consumer dynamics; attention to a death-related storybook, novel, or nonfictional work in a section on reading or literature; consideration of conceptual and ethical issues related to definition of death, suicide, or euthanasia in a contemporary issues or honors seminar; or research on epitaphs and burial customs in a social science class. Integration of death education in these ways into the broader curriculum does not necessarily dilute or fragment its integrity. Rather, it follows the principle that topics related to death are to be found throughout the spectrum of living. Also, brief exposures to death-related topics may be less threatening—particularly for younger students—and these exposures may prepare the way for fuller and more explicit treatment at a later level. Finally, while cumbersome formal procedures are often required to gain approval for a full-scale course on death and dying, that may not be the case for less ambitious curricular initiatives or for the implementation of discretionary options within an existing curricular program.

Although programs of formal instruction like these, or variations such as church discussion groups, are valuable in themselves, they do not exhaust opportunities for helping with death education. Education is not confined to the limited time frames of the classroom; and events in life that impinge on the community, the home, the school, or the individual child can have power and potential far exceeding traditional forms of pedagogy. Such events can inspire at least two additional forms of death education. The first has been called "the teachable moment." This is an opportunity created by an event that stimulates cognitive inquiry in a relatively nonthreatening way. It might involve a child who finds a small dead animal in the woods and comes home to ask about the experience, the death in a school of a plant or animal for whom no particular attachment has developed, or a report concerning a public figure, such as a president or some other prominent person whose status is widely recognized yet who is distant. Some of these opportunities may be anticipated, though most will simply arise in the normal course of events without prior warning. Some can be worked into school, home, or other interactions as real-life examples of ongoing discussions. Others inspire such curiosity or have such significance for learning that they warrant interrupting whatever else is going on. Cases of this last sort can be so insistent that adults are rightly said to fail in their duties to children if they gloss over them or refuse to respond appropriately.

A second form of the insistent death-related life event is that which is emotionally disturbing to the child (and perhaps also to the adults) whom it touches. One might call this "a nurturing moment." I am thinking here of occasions when normal people are upset in such a way that they need an opportunity to vent and share feelings and to gain support from familiar people around them. The death of a playmate or peer in school, of a friend in the neighborhood, or a relative or family member can excite strong emotions in a child. Parents and other adults (who may themselves be grieving) must appreciate the child's need for security and support in such moments and must be particularly sensitive so as not to intensify anxiety, confusion, or isolation through word or deed. In these contexts, those who send a child away or who urge others not to talk to the child about the death must learn that this does not erase the reality with which he or she must deal. In fact, such behavior only withdraws the assistance of a caring community precisely when that is most needed. The school that suspends classes after the death of a student at least recognizes that sometimes we cannot go on with business as usual when death intrudes. It is only a logical extension of that negative point to come to the realization that we also have a positive duty to help children cope with such unfortunate events. We must, in other words, learn to use even death as an opportunity for growth in children. To fail to grow is to fall back, and death can be a very important occasion for learning how to deal constructively with the problems of life. We neglect that only at the risk of failing our children precisely when they most need us.

Responsibilities

Adults who seek to take up opportunities such as those described above should first realize what is required for the endeavor. Four sorts of responsibilities might be suggested as incumbent on those who intend or expect to become engaged in some kind of death education with children. (Note that such a description really applies to all of us because no one who has anything to do with children can really avoid such an engagement indefinitely.) The first of these responsibilities is *preparation*. We are more likely to be successful and to be comfortable with interactions that we have anticipated at least in some measure and with those to which we have given some forethought. Preparation may not guarantee success, and it may not call for a formal or explicit process in those whose life experiences or native endowments already serve this purpose. But for most people in our society it is a helpful and even a necessary prerequisite. Preparation for helping with death education is mainly of two sorts: (1) initiating reflection on one's own thoughts and feelings about death and (2) a study of relevant content in the field of death, dying, and bereavement.

It is often said to parents and members of the helping professions that they should not undertake interactions related to death with children, patients, or other vulnerable groups until they have first come to terms with their own concepts, attitudes, and needs in this area. There is an important truth

contained in such directives, but (as here) this truth is usually
not articulated precisely and thus may discourage good workers
before they even begin. This underlying truth is that all relationships are at least two-sided. Hence, the outlook of the adult
helper is always an operative factor in the relationship. It is
particularly important to recognize this when the relationship
concerns death, a topic that touches each of us deeply and in
multiple ways. To believe otherwise is to neglect omnipresent
concerns for one's own mortality. One cannot expect to operate
from a wholly neutral or disengaged stance when interacting
with children about death.

It is equally true, however, that one cannot operate from a
finished or perfected stance. This is the misstatement or over-
exaggeration in the way in which such advice is typically given
or received. No one ever comes to terms with death within this
life in such a final way that there is nothing left to do. Living
always offers some potential for advancing and deepening one's
appreciation of the significance of death. That is the implication
of Kastenbaum's tongue-in-cheek title "We Covered Death
Today" (8). Finality is not an achievable goal in dealing with
death. What is essential is initiating a process of reflection and
self-discovery, not finishing it.

In addition to preparing in an ongoing way in this first
sense, helpers also need to acquaint themselves with relevant
content in the field of death, dying, and bereavement. Over the
past 20 years, the literature and other resources in this field
have grown tremendously (3). Few need or will be able to
master the field as a whole, or even the broad subarea of
children and death. But, again, one can make a beginning, and
the improvement in available resources of all sorts is encourag-
ing. In this regard, the adjective "relevant" has two sorts of
implications. First, general knowledge of some topics such as the
historical-cultural situation of children and death in our society,
the development of death-related thoughts and feelings during
childhood, and the impact of environment and life experiences,
is necessary in some measure for all adults who seek to interact
with children. Such knowledge is available (e.g., 9). Second,
other more specific topics are relevant especially for particular
situations, for instance, an understanding of bereavement patterns

for dealing with a child who has experienced a death in the family or some insight into coping techniques for helping a child with a long-term terminal illness.*

In this book, we have attempted to provide a broad and helpful base from which to begin. We do not, however, subscribe to the overenthusiastic blurb that appeared on one earlier book for teachers, claiming that "with no special training, you can teach death education as easily as you teach the basics" (10). (Which educators would find that to be a responsible claim in their own primary fields?) Instead, we urge as full and as rich as exploitation of our subject as may be possible before beginning this task—and continuing thereafter—and I try to show in this chapter how additional self-study and formal preparation might be undertaken.

The second responsibility for helpers is to respond to real needs in children. This may seem obvious, but all too often inter-generational dialogue is hampered when adults do not make a sincere and effective effort to identify and to satisfy the real concerns that are animating children. John Dewey said somewhere that there must be something wrong with schools that bore pupils instead of capitalizing on their native curiosity. Much the same is true of a society that inhibits rather than encourages constructive death education. Responses that do not engage with real needs only frustrate children and discourage them from coming back to such sources in the future. We can become effective responders only by improving our awareness of developmental and environmental factors that relate to childhood and death and by listening in an active way to the concerns of each particular child. Knowledge about developmental and environmental factors in children's death concerns provides a broad framework for interactions with children,† although it never substitutes for careful attention to an individual child. In the general field of death and dying; in programs like hospice, which care for dying people and their families; and in interactions involving children, almost nothing is more important than *active listening*.

*These subjects are dealt with more fully in H. Wass and C. A. Corr (Eds.), *Childhood and death,* forthcoming from Hemisphere.

†The most recent presentation of such knowledge can be found in ibid., chaps. 1 and 2.

Following determination of the real needs of an individual child, the third responsibility for helpers is to communicate effectively. Once adults have heard the child fully and accurately, they must then insure that the child hears them in a similar way. This reception of messages needs to take place at four primary levels: cognitive, affective, behavioral, and valuational. Above all, from a cognitive, or intellectual, standpoint adults must insure that what they say is true. It need not be the whole of the truth as they know it, and it must never be delivered in a thoughtless or brutal fashion. But to be effective communicators, adults must believe in what they say to children. No adult is infallible, and we would probably be better off to acknowledge more often that we do not have an answer or that we have made a mistake. Still, messages that go out to children should not knowingly be based on misinformation, deception, and lies, or be clouded with irrelevant information. Examples of such faulty communications are all too easy to find. Adults who translate death into the language of sleep, who rush out to buy a new guppy to replace a dead fish before their child comes home to find it gone, who hide a death by pretending that the person has moved far away, who claim that someone died because God loved that person and wanted to have her with Him, or who simply give a complex spiritual or theological answer to a simple concrete or biologic question—all are guilty of this sort of faulty communicaton.

At the affective level, one needs to permit children to vent strong feelings and to bring anxiety and guilt out into the open where they can be seen in proper perspective and dealt with accordingly. For this, we need to keep in mind that truth, no matter how bad it is, is almost always less frightening than the demons that will be conjured up in our own psyches. Strong feelings can themselves become a source of trauma when they are merely suppressed and not properly dealt with. Guilt is often unfounded or dependent on unreliable, magical thinking. Moreover, even where truth does not dissipate the underlying reality, sharing a truth can mitigate its emotional overlay. A private hell feeds on itself and increases, whereas a shared anxiety often decreases.

This process is not one-sided; adults can often provide

support merely by sharing their own feelings of sadness, loss, and uncertainty. Even the act of gathering a child into one's lap to offer an explanation that may not be fully understood shows concern and demonstrates that the child need not continue to struggle alone. And every teacher or counselor knows that constituting a group of peers to talk out a problem creates a network of support in which children themselves can be the most effective helpers of their classmates. Adults often hesitate in these tasks because they assume that if they begin such work they will have to have "answers" or appropriate responses for anything that may arise. This is shortsighted because it fails to perceive that children are often their own best helpers and that it is usually quite productive merely to show that we care, are sincere, and are willing to join a common endeavor to resolve the problem.

Within the behavioral arena, adults need to recall that many of the most significant lessons they themselves learned come through bodily behavior and not just words. Children can conclude that death is an undesirable or disreputable topic when adults neglect it or shun it systematically. Worse yet, young people can be taught to misunderstand their own needs as whole persons and members of a community when they are surrounded by adults who take no notice of a death and who refuse to take part in funeral practices. Miseducation of this sort ought to be rejected; instead, we should follow the guidance of Jackson, who has long advocated the value of acting out strong feelings, of using ceremonial ritual to confirm the solidarity and continuity of life, and of permitting children to share in adult experiences (11, 12). A simple illustration of Jackson's viewpoint might be seen in the case of a small child who is permitted to bury a pet fish or turtle that has died and to emulate an adult funeral service. But this advice applies not only after a death. One college student invited several young neighborhood children to help with her "homework" for the university. The help involved no more than visiting a cemetery with her and discussing their reactions. Because the task was presented in a positive and nonthreatening manner, the children were eager to cooperate; and they benefited in many ways from an experience they might otherwise not have had. On-site visits to a funeral home, a mausoleum or crematory, a hospice, or other death-related institutions could have similar results.

A final realm for effective communication is that of values. Because adults are sometimes unclear about their own values in relation to death or are unsure of appropriate ways to impart values, they often hold back from direct engagement with children in this dimension. The false assumption is that fundamental values can be kept apart from everyday interactions with life and death. In fact, basic attitudes and values appear in all of our conduct toward death, even in whether or not we admit that topic into our thoughts and deeds. Thus, it is not only church groups who can engage in the teaching of beliefs concerning death. Parents can impart the values that they prize, and even the public schools can teach about beliefs that bear on the significance of death. The main point is to acknowledge the importance of helping children to acquire a value framework that takes death into account. To help children acquire such a framework, adults must avoid conveying values about which they have no real conviction. Thus, religious stories are often misused as handy "explanations" by adults who have not thought out their own positions. In contast, helpers who are secure in their own values will be able to provide children the freedom and the encouragement they need to learn to cope with death. One cannot "protect" young people from death-related encounters and explorations throughout their childhood years and still expect them to emerge as adults who are adequately equipped to cope with life.

The fourth responsibility that falls on helpers is cooperation. Actually, this responsibility emerges from what has gone before. Thoughts, feelings, behaviors, and values—the salient aspects of what we might broadly term *encounters with death*—will arise throughout life. They cannot be restricted to a specific time or context. One cannot expect that death need only be mentioned in Sunday school or that it can be encapsulated in a particular course or that an "expert" in the field will always be available and appropriate. No one has an exclusive corner on wisdom about death. Children often learn more from their own private experiences and from their peers than they do from adults, but they draw most effectively on those adults with whom they feel close and comfortable, regardless of official labels or roles. We can anticipate the best results when children and their peers are allowed to work together in an ongoing process of death education with parents, teachers, counselors, the clergy, care givers, and all of the other relevant adults and institutions in our society. Our effort in this book is to stimulate such constructive cooperation, to show that it is a feasible project, and to provide both guidelines and resources for its implementation.

Goals

Knott (7) has suggested that death education of all sorts may be understood as involving a triad of overlapping concerns: information sharing, values clarification, and coping behaviors. I think Knott is correct both in identifying these three as basic areas of concern and in noting that they usually interweave in practice. All death education involves a process of sharing information, an attempt to identify values that underlie feelings and actions, and an effort to develop behaviors to cope with the ways in which death impinges on life. A particular program may emphasize one or another of these focuses, but all will be present in some degree, for the implications of death run both deep and broad.

If we apply Knott's three concerns to helping children and set this in the light of our preceding analysis of adult responsibilities, we can restate what has been said in the form of goals for helpers. Perhaps the most fundamental thing that children—and all the rest of us—need to do is to find a way to cope with whatever life presents. Such presentations are of two sorts: those arising from within us, from our own inner needs, and those coming from outside, from encounters with the world. For example, the former might involve a need to be reassured of our own security against a possible threat of loss or separation; the latter might require us to deal with a puzzling or frightening event in the course of our daily affairs. The most basic task for a sound program of death education is to assist children to find effective ways of satisfying such needs—at least insofar as they relate to death. Whatever we have to offer by way of information, feelings, or values will all go for naught if it does not result in or cannot be related to constructive coping.

In fact, however, when we set that goal clearly before us, everything else then falls into place. Functional coping is fostered, initially, by allowing a child to release, share, or explore strong feelings about death. Second, functional coping depends on the acquisition of reliable information and the gaining of relevant experiences. Third, it depends on the testing of our ideas and the exchange of viewpoints or interpretations with others. Fourth, it leads to the identification and the formation of values that can subsequently serve as principles to guide further decisions and actions. All of these aspects, in other words, feed back into and improve our ongoing coping with living.

Another way to view death education has been suggested by the French cultural historian Philippe Ariès (13). Looking back on a time when death was a prominent and recognized feature of life, Ariès offered the following observation:

> Men of that period were profoundly and rapidly socialized. The family did not intervene to delay the socialization of the child. Moreover, socialization did not separate man from nature, with which he could not interfere short of a miracle. (p. 28)

All children undergo a process of socialization as they grow into adulthood and prepare to cope with life in a mature and responsible way. The problem in our society with those aspects of the socialization process that relate to death is that so many of them retard the growth of children and do not prepare them to engage with central dimensions of human existence. We confuse ignorance with innocence, suppression of honest feelings with contentment, segregation with the need to try out behavior patterns, and facile stories with careful value formation. Most of this is little more than misguided protectionism. Adults do not intend harm for their children and many do better than this catalog of thanatological sins would suggest. But too many of us unwittingly are our own and our children's worst enemies. Parenthood does entail safeguarding our children, but that must be accomplished in a thoughtful way and one that looks to the future. We do not help children by avoiding or squelching overt, temporary distress; instead, we should capitalize on it to achieve ultimate mastery and growth. In other words, adults must see their roles in the light of a sensible appreciation of children's needs. Responsible death education—education for life and living—is one of those needs for every child who is preparing to assume his or her rightful roles as a mature person, a member of the social community, and a citizen of the universe.

Preparation for Helping

Formal Programs

A wide variety of programs to prepare adults for helping in death education with children is possible. Programs may range from two-hour lecture-discussions in a course on death and dying and short presentations to lay and professional audiences, through one-day and two-week workshops, to full-scale courses exclusively devoted to the subject of children and death. One might also think of ongoing church discussion groups on this subject or of a series of interrelated presentations sponsored by a civic, educational, or religious organization. We cannot consider all such programs here, but it is helpful at least to suggest that there are many possible options for preparing helpers. I regard the day-long workshop and the full-scale college course as the most basic of all these options because they provide sufficient scope to do a satisfactory job and because most of the other formats can be seen as extracts from or condensations of these two. My emphasis here is on the day-long workshop because it is more common and because the full-scale college course on children and death is not yet a widely recognized model.

Elsehwere (14) I have outlined a number of patterns for day-long workshops on children and death. Every workshop must be geared to the needs of its particular audience, the resources available, and the capacities of its staff. But all have some common threads. The format, is usually four or five 60- to 90-minute sessions with ample time for questions and discussion, short breaks, and meals. Normally, they require little more logistics than a blackboard and a motion-picture or slide projector. But these are largely externals. True communality in such programs can be seen in their essential elements as reflected in a schematic outline and in the description that might be used to announce the workshop. The latter could be phrased in the following way: This workshop is designed to sensitize adults to problems involving children and death in our society; to examine research concerning the formation of death-related concepts and attitudes in childhood and adolescence; and to recommend strategies and resources adults can use to help children understand and deal with death more effectively.

In a four-session workshop, the opening session should be used to introduce the participants, to identify their backgrounds and the issues that concern them, and to begin an exploration of their own early contacts with and present attitudes toward death. The aim is not to complete the last exploration but only to introduce it as a topic for discussion. That reaffirms the operational relevancy of the adult's own death-related encounters and attitudes in all interactions with children, and it opens the way to an investigation of death-related needs in childhood. Another quite compatible way of achieving understanding and legitimization of childhood needs is to approach them through an account of typical death-related experiences and attitudes in our society and of the ways in which these are likely to influence children. Previously (4, 15), I have argued that one can characterize this society's typical experiential pattern as involving limited contact with natural human death, extensive fantasization of death through media presentations, and an increasing proportion of human-caused deaths. That pattern seems to correlate with a rather large share of discomfort, ambivalence, and distancing in our attitudes toward death. The result is a lot of misguided protectionism from adults that attempts to hide death from children through such practices as physical segregation, denial, and evasive or confusing language patterns. If we isolate these behaviors from their normal milieu, their limitations and the defects in their underlying motivations are readily apparent.

The second session of a workshop of this sort properly focuses on what can be said about the formation of death-related concepts and attitudes in childhood and adolescence. Research on this topic of even the earliest or simplest sort demonstrates that normal children do begin to have thoughts and feelings about death at an early age, certainly by the preschool or nursery school years (16). It is important to recognize that learning to deal with death is a part of the child's overall development in learning to deal with life. Hence, it is the development of the child's total psyche that is of concern, not just one or the other aspect; and environmental factors or life experiences are just as relevant as internal processes or capacities. This topic is central to any educational or interaction program that is concerned with children. It need not be belabored; the aim is education for use by ordinary adults, not merely specialists. The aim is satisfied even if the audience gains only a general sense of the relevant patterns and factors that come into question—as long as they also perceive the concomitant moral, which is that we must listen carefully to the concerns of each individual child before we attempt a response or impose our own agenda.

On the basis of this last discussion, the third session of the workshop might lay down some general guidelines for interacting with children. Many of these have already been set forth, for example: Listen and respond to real needs; insure that whatever you say is true; permit release and acting out of strong feelings; provide sympathetic support, acceptance, and reassurance; make good use of community and ceremonial rituals; share value frameworks in which there is real conviction; and work cooperatively in an integrating way, taking advantage of all of the enriching influences in a child's life. General strategies for curricular and teaching programs or for responding to the "teachable moment" could also be considered here. Throughout, it is good to keep in mind that, in many ways, the details of these guidelines and strategies are not so important; what really counts is their overall shape or orientation. The desired outcome is a constructive attitude, not a set of quick tricks or manipulative devices. And the underlying theme is that all of this is well within the grasp of an ordinary, mature adult.

Finally, a fourth session can identify a good resource guide (3) and different types of resources (discussed more fully below). It would also be desirable to give examples of many kinds of resources and to show how each can be used to best advantage. One might even select for detailed evaluation those resources that are especially suitable for a particular audience or in a specific setting. We need no overwhelm participants with bibliography or mediography, but a short list of various types of recommended materials is always useful as something to take home from the workshop. If a fifth or additional session is possible, it might address special concerns of the participants or special cases that are either the most likely to occur or the most difficult to handle.

Self-study Programs

In a new field where historically there have not been many experts, few who now teach or write for adults have themselves been trained in formal programs of death education. More often than not, they have taken advantage of whatever instruction and resources were available; exploited their own existing knowledge, experience, and skills; and taught themselves much of what they now know. As they continue to share and discuss their insights, candor demands recognition that they acquire many ideas, suggestions, and materials from students and others with whom they come in contact. I say this to emphasize the importance of self-study and ongoing informal dialogue. It is quite foolish to think, as many seem to do, that one can only learn something by enrolling in a course or that formal credentials are an exclusive mark of wisdom, especially when the object of that wisdom is a fundamental and enduring aspect of the human condition. Those who enter a program of self-study need to be encouraged and assisted, not denigrated and frustrated by arbitrary barriers.

Because self-study programs are most often individual plans or spontaneous inquiry groups of no more than a very few people, they need not have a very rigid syllabus and they do not lend themselves to much generalization. What distinguishes self-study is not so much its content as its manner of organization, and perhaps also its resources. Those working on their own can march each to her or his own drummer, though they often must make use of instruments and music that are readily at hand. As far as content goes, in the previous section I have outlined some patterns for a day-long workshop in great detail partly to identify topics that could also be applicable to self-study. Obviously, an informal program of personal study could benefit by addressing topics the same as or similar to those taken up in a formal course organized by others. I can illustrate this by rephrasing five goals of the formal workshop as guidelines or objectives for a program of independent study.

The first is to sensitize adults to their own needs and to the needs that children have in dealing with death. Some adults explicitly deny that children have needs related to death; others appear to act on unarticulated but similar assumptions; and still another group is merely unconvinced of the existence of such needs. These adults may or may not acknowledge their own death-related needs, although these needs may be in part the source of their views concerning needs or lack thereof that they attribute to children. Here, the goal is to encourage an un-obscured sensitivity to the reality of death as a significant factor in human life, whether in adulthood or in childhood. Paradox-ically, that objective is often best achieved when death is shrunk from the outsized proportions generated by unfamiliarity and anxiety to its normal role in life. Death education is a process of bringing the elements of life back into harmony, not one of sensationalizing or overemphasizing an object of special interest or special pleading. Of course, those who take up a program of self-study may already be sensitized to death-related needs in themselves and in children. But sensitivity can become dulled, and we need to be alert to the importance of maintaining its keenness.

A second objective for independent study is to realize how death-related needs are influenced by the way in which our society experiences and copes with death, and in particular to appreciate how adult viewpoints and behaviors can influence children's perspectives in favorable and unfavorable ways. This objective carries us from the timeless abstraction of general needs to the concrete idiosyncrasies of a specified historical and cultural context. Death is actually always encountered in a particular context of life, and the nature of that context will inevitably shape the encounter. Further, within any designated society one can identify typical ways in which adults interact with children in regard to death. Because the overall patterns of encounters with death in our society are so distinctive—being quite limited in their realistic qualities and heavily distorted by selectivity and fantasization—we need to understand these patterns and to come to see how they often lead to common adult behaviors that are dysfunctional for children. By exposing inadequacies in need fulfillment, death education prepares the way in this objective for new relationships between adults and children based on more productive coping strategies.

A third goal for our program is to examine recent research and theories on the formation of death-related concepts and attitudes in childhood and adolescence. Even those who deny or are skeptical of death-related needs in early childhood must admit that at *some* point children are capable of considering death and begin to think and have feelings about it. An observant outsider might infer from common adult behavior that this point is not reached until the child has come to adulthood or otherwise left the protective environment of the familial greenhouse to encounter the harsh outside world. But this is patently false, so explicit pronouncements tend to put the watershed at an earlier and often arbitrarily designated age. Thus, in speaking of the young child, Ross says that "there is little need in his spring-green world for an understanding of the dead" (17, p. 250). Unfortunately for this viewpoint, the body of available research demonstrates that children do begin to draw inferences, form concepts, and develop feelings about death at quite an early age (18–20). Inferences may be founded on an inadequate experiential base; concepts may be incomplete; and feelings may be disproportioned or misfocused—but all are real and cannot wisely be dismissed out of hand. Death education should develop a knowledge base for helpers that respects developmental and environmental factors in childhood as well as the uniqueness of the individual child.

A fourth goal for self-study is to learn ways in which helpers should conduct themselves to foster in children a healthy attitude toward death. We need not limit ourselves to identifying flaws or to prohibiting undesirable forms of behavior. There are constructive modes of conduct both in identifying opportunities for death education with children and in responding to such occasions. Conduct with regard to death does not lend itself to cookbook recipes or simplistic formulas, but that need not frustrate conversation or prohibit interactions with children. A positive orientation can be developed that is applicable both to informal education in the home or community and to more formal education in the schools. Death education can aim adults in the right direction without preempting the uniqueness of each encounter with a child or the individual tactics that might suit a special situation.

The final goal for independent study is to learn about resources for use in working with children. Many well-intentioned adults are sympathetic to the needs of children and to contexts of interaction, and they are willing to try to learn about childhood development and a prospectus for their own behavior. But at that point, they often feel abandoned. Lacking knowledge of available materials, they feel as if they have been set adrift on a treacherous sea with only their own wits and words to aid them. Undoubtedly, one can do much with nature itself and a little imagination. Still, unnecessary limitations need not be applauded. Many sorts of resources and many good aids are at hand. Individual adults can select those that are most suitable to their situation if they know where and how to look and what to look for. Awareness of available resources can reinforce constructive behavior by suggesting options in methods and materials, and even in topics, that may not previously have been appreciated. Thus, a comprehensive program of formal or informal death education will see resources as an integral component of the whole, rather than as an optional appendix. In the next section I provide an introduction to relevant sorts of resources, and particular instances follow in the section of the text, "Resources."

Resources for Helping

The one great resource for death education with children that we all share in common is life itself. Our everyday experiences are full of "little deaths," the small separations and losses or beginnings and endings that mark change and growth. These events can teach us all a great deal about death. We need only be sensitive to them and keep in mind the organizing standard of our overriding concern for helping children with death education. Further, there are at least three other primary sorts of resources that can benefit adults and be employed with profit by them for the purposes of death education. These are printed materials, audiovisual items, and organizations in the community. I do not identify individual items here, preferring instead to concentrate on the types of resources available and their potential uses.

There are several sorts of printed materials that can be useful for death education with children. The most obvious are books, which may themselves be intended primarily for adults, for children, or for joint reading. Death education books are beginning to achieve new levels of sophistication. Many early titles in the field were uneven and overconfident. They promised too much and delivered too little. We had much to learn before this subject could be treated with authority. Indeed, there is still room for improvement, but now the literature for adults as described in Chapter 5 includes 44 titles that span fictional or autobiographical first-person encounters with death; studies of conceptual development and coping with dying or bereavement; and compendiums of advice for parents, counselors, and teachers. Adults can now find some discussion of almost any topic related to death education in one of these books.

Recently, there have been published what amount to freestanding bibliographies, books that describe other books in the field of death and dying. Mainly, these bibliographies concern themselves with literature for children and are intended for use by adults. These books demonstrate the rapid development during the past few years of a rather large body of death-related literature for children. Of course, in one form or another, death has long been a part of oral and written traditions for children; but it has recently become more central to plot and character development in many stories. Some of these are avowedly didactic, moralistic, or pedagogical in character. They seek to provide information, to inculcate values, or to teach children something about death. Perhaps the more successful are those in which death in some of its many manifestations is simply part of the tale. These range from the simplest picture books and stories for beginning readers to the most elegant and imaginative works for older children. By reintegrating death with life within their covers, such books teach the most important lesson of all, and they respond to the child's natural spectrum of interests and experiences. Not all are equally well written or suitable to every child, but Wass's descriptions of 155 titles in Chapter 6 gives ample room for selection in theme, treatment, and style.

Some writers (e.g., 21) commend the use of children's literature as "bibliotherapy," a kind of therapeutic or constructive intervention in the lives of children through books. Whatever we think of this concept, it is obvious that books can have an important value for children. All printed materials, but especially imaginative literature of the best kind, can stimulate a child's creative tendencies, enlarge horizons, confirm human solidarity in the face of difficulties, and foster critical assessment. Adults can capitalize on these possibilities by acquainting themselves with the panorama of death-related literature that is now in print and by making some of the best titles available for children. With a little guidance, children will begin to see how they can entertain and eduate themselves through such titles. Of course, it helps if the adults have also looked through the books so that they are prepared for the sorts of questions that a particular story might stimulate.

Some read-along books are specifically designed to be explored by children and adults together. Usually, these tell the simplest stories and are meant for the youngest children. The idea is to create an environment of sharing. To this end, the book is merely an instrument; it is not indispensable and should never become a handicap to free exchange. Although content is important, many children enjoy and profit from the very process of a shared reading or a period of story telling. Many books can be used in this way, particularly those with an interesting story and some attractive illustrations. The only point that may seem new or unusual in all this is my contention that a death-related story can serve as well as many others. But that need not be surprising; for if the essential element is that of sharing, then the object of concern can just as well be a tale of sadness and loss as one of happiness and success. Reading to a child about the death of a pet or the life cycle of a tree may prompt unexpected disclosures that might otherwise have gone unexpressed or unexplored.

Printed resources of a quite different sort are to be found in a few specialized periodicals and a wide range of journal articles. Casual readers often see little more than the popular magazines of the home, a grocery check-out counter, or a physician's waiting room. Even these occasionally print a death-related story, though often it will lack much depth or substance. But helpers should know that nearly every field of special interest has its own supportive periodicals. Many of these that are concerned with children have published during the last 10 or 15 years at least some articles that touch on death education. Interested adults can identify such pieces through the usual indexes to such periodicals or through a good bibliographic guide. A reference librarian can often point out a helpful index or abstracting service for a particular field. Beyond that, within the field of death and dying itself there are three prominent periodicals: *Omega,* an early journal with a slant toward the behavioral sciences; the Canadian journal *Essence;* and *Death Education.* Adults who are interested in death education have much to gain from a quick survey of these sorts of periodical resources.

In addition to printed materials, there are many audiovisuals that can be employed to good effect in death education for children. Films, filmstrips, records, tapes, or cassettes can have particular value for youngsters who may not yet have well-developed reading skills. Audiovisuals can also complement the written word and, in some cases, may exceed its power because of their broad sensory appeal. All too often, adults neglect audiovisual resources because they fear this power when linked to the subject of death and because they are unaware of their accessibility. Certainly, some audiovisuals about death are very powerful and should not be presented to unprepared or unsupported audiences. But that is hardly more than to say that no resource, however good in its own right, should ever be used in a thoughtless or indiscriminate way. A film can be death-related if it does no more than portray a life cycle, and it can be no more threatening than a portrait of a gentle encounter between some children and a dead animal. As for availability, Pacholski's annotated listing of audiovisual materials in Chapter 7 gives 143 titles with descriptions and a topical index. Pacholski rightly reminds us that many of these audiovisuals may also be available through local public, educational, and other resource centers or organizations. Helpers who invest time and energy in searching out such resources can often save money and simultaneously enrich the opportunities that follow for the education of children.

Finally, no list of resources would be complete that did not mention the many community and specialized organizations that are to be found in every local area. Most of these organizations will willingly share their expertise, printed materials, and audiovisuals with interested adults and young people. I have been most grateful to draw on such organizations in my own classes and workshops, whether for children or for adults. Most organizations are in turn pleased to make known their interests and to advertise their goals to members of the community. The very existence of these organizations confirms again the omnipresence of death-related resources in the social and everyday fabric of life all around us.

Helping the Helpers

I close this essay with a short caution about those who would conduct programs of death education for adults to prepare them for helping children. As of this writing, the Forum for Death Education and Counseling is the one national organization in North America that is struggling to develop training programs and criteria for identifying competency among those who teach in the area of death and dying. At the moment, few programs of this sort and no recognized criteria yet exist. This means that almost anyone can announce or conduct a program of death education. That freedom has made possible many valuable initiatives and many constructive programs, but it brings with it a need to scrutinize carefully qualifications in this popular field. Simply to have worked in some aspect of death, dying, or bereavement does not guarantee that one has a sound grasp on the field as a whole or that one is an effective educator. Nevertheless, sufficient time has now passed and sufficient opportunities are now available for writing, publishing, and teaching, that it is not improper to expect a history of accomplishment from most people. Even then, it would be wise to talk with a person at length to explore his or her creativity and flexibility and to insure that the planned educational program will serve the needs for which it is intended.

References

1. Pine, V. R. A socio-historical portrait of death education. *Death Education*, 1977, *1*, 57–84.
2. Feifel, H. (Ed.). *The meaning of death.* New York: McGraw-Hill, 1959.
3. Wass, H., Corr, C. A., Pacholski, R. A., & Sanders, C. M. *Death education: An annotated resource guide.* Washington: Hemisphere, 1980.
4. Corr, C. A. A model syllabus for death and dying courses. *Death Education*, 1978, *1*, 433–457.
5. Leviton, D. Death education. In H. Feifel (Ed.), *New meanings of death.* New York: McGraw-Hill, 1977, pp. 253–272.
6. Leviton, D. The scope of death education. *Death Education*, 1977, *1*, 41–45.
7. Knott, J. E. Death education for all. In H. Wass (Ed.), *Dying: Facing the facts.* Washington: Hemisphere, 1979, pp. 385–403.
8. Kastenbaum, R. We covered death today. *Death Education*, 1977, *1*, 85–92.
9. Wass, H. (Ed.). *Dying: Facing the facts.* Washington: Hemisphere, 1979.
10. Stanford, G., & Perry, D. *Death out of the closet: A curriculum guide to living with dying.* New York: Bantam, 1976.
11. Jackson, E. N. *Telling a child about death.* New York: Hawthorn, 1965.
12. Jackson, E. N. Bereavement and grief. In H. Wass (Ed.), *Dying: Facing the facts.* Washington: Hemisphere, 1979, pp. 256–281.
13. Ariès, P. *Western attitudes toward death: From the Middle Ages to the present* (P. Ranum, Trans.). Baltimore: Johns Hopkins University Press, 1974.
14. Corr, C. A. Workshops on children and death. *Essence*, 1980, *4*, 5–18.
15. Corr, C. Reconstructing the changing face of death. In H. Wass (Ed.), *Dying: Facing the facts.* Washington: Hemisphere, 1979, pp. 5–43.
16. Stillion, J., & Wass, H. Children and death. In H. Wass (Ed.), *Dying: Facing the facts.* Washington: Hemisphere, 1979, 208–235.

17. Ross, E. S. Children's books relating to death: A discussion. In E. A. Grollman (Ed.), *Explaining death to children.* Boston: Beacon, 1967, pp. 249-271.
18. Kastenbaum, R. Death and development through the lifespan. In H. Feifel (Ed.), *New meanings of death.* New York: McGraw-Hill, 1977, pp. 17-45.
19. Kastenbaum, R. *Death, society, and human experience.* St. Louis: Mosby, 1977, pp. 114-134.
20. Lonetto, R. *Children's conceptions of death.* New York: Springer, 1980.
21. Bernstein, J. E. *Books to help children cope with separation and loss.* New York: Bowker, 1977, esp. pp. 20-39.

RESOURCES

∞∞∞

BOOKS FOR ADULTS:
AN ANNOTATED BIBLIOGRAPHY

∞∞∞

CHARLES A. CORR

The bibliography that follows describes 44 books for adults that are in some way related to helping children cope with death. This listing is restricted to book-length entries, as distinct from journal or periodical articles, because the former are judged more likely to be of substantial and enduring value. Readers should be aware of the journal literature, however, and those with special interests might wish to explore its potential. That can most easily be undertaken by consulting the annotated descriptions of literature concerning death education and the references to death-related bibliographies in the resource guide prepared by Wass and her colleagues and described in this bibliography.

The present bibliography is intended to be both selective and representative. That is, the titles listed here have been chosen from among the available book-length literature either because they most deserve to be recommended to readers or because they have achieved some prominence and require comment. At the same time, these choices are also designed to reflect examples of each principal type of work and to include major topical areas within the field, such as analyses of various types of loss; first-person accounts, either biographical or fictional; and treatments of developmental, educational, counseling, and biblio-graphic considerations. In view of this breadth, I hope that those who examine this bibliography will be able to get a quick sense of the range and depth of books available for helping children cope with death.

Each entry in the bibliography contains a short description of the contents of the book in question. Few people will need

77

or be able to read all of the books mentioned here. Nevertheless, by skimming over these descriptions, readers can save time and determine for themselves which titles to seek out for more leisurely exploration in the light of particular interests. Where it seems helpful, annotations include information about an author's background or a brief evaluation of a book's special strengths or weaknesses.

Some books can be read with profit both by older children or adolescents and by adults. Others are designed to be read together by young children and adults. In such cases, the same title may appear both here and in Chapter 6. Where that occurs, the annotations will naturally be similar, although one may emphasize the book's value for adults while the other relates it to children.

Agee, J. *A death in the family.* New York: Grosset & Dunlap, 1967; Bantam, 1969. This Pulitzer Prize-winning novel describes the sudden and unexpected death of Jay Follet and the impact of that event on his family. The scenes in which six-year-old Rufus and his younger sister Catherine attempt to make sense out of what has happened are rich with insight into the ways in which children often misunderstand and are misunderstood by the adults around them. The scene is Tennessee early in this century, but the themes are timeless. Every adult can benefit from Agee's masterful evocation of the children's perspective in which we see clearly the problems that they have in dealing with their feelings and in framing questions to resolve their confusion.

Anthony, S. *The discovery of death in childhood and after.* New York: Basic, 1972. This book is described by its publisher as "an enlarged and thoroughly revised version" of the book published in 1940 under the title *The child's discovery of death: A study in child psychology.* The original book was based on research conducted in England between 1937 and 1939, but it has long been out of print and difficult to obtain. In general, it favored a developmental theory of death-related concepts but insisted that they are closely associated with other ideas and factors and that the idea of death occurs very readily in the fantasies of normal children.

The author sees the revised version as "repeating and adding to earlier observations, relating them to later researches in kindred fields, placing the whole in the sort of setting such a subject deserves" (p. 12). In other words, the revised version is more accessible, more up to date, and more concerned with a broad cultural perspective. A classic text that shows influences from Freud and Piaget and that is of some importance for specialists.

Berg, D. W., & Daugherty, G. G. *The individual, society and death: An anthology of readings.* DeKalb, Ill.: Perspectives on Death, 1972. This is an example of the scissors-and-paste approach to anthologizing snippets from many diverse sources. The text is part of a package for high school students, which also includes the *Student Activity Book* and *Teacher's Resource Book.* Perhaps the earliest entry of its type in the field, this private publication is just the sort of approach to death education that we need now to put behind us.

Bernstein, J. E. *Books to help children cope with separation and loss.* New York: Bowker, 1977. As the title indicates, the scope of this bibliographic resource is much broader than the field of death, dying, and bereavement. Part I deals with the use of books to help children and with the concept of bibliotherapy; Part II provides an annotated bibliography of 438 books for children that address themes of separation (new siblings, schools, neighborhoods, etc.), loss (death, divorce, or marital separation; desertion; serious illness; war; and displacement), and security (who will take care of me?—foster care, stepparents, adoption, and homelessness); and Part III adds unannotated selected lists of readings for adults on separation and loss and on bibliotherapy. There are indexes by author, title, subject, interest level, and reading level. This is a rich and unparalleled resource. The section on death alone fills almost 50 pages and offers paragraph-length descriptions and evaluations of 112 titles.

Bernstein, J. E. *Loss and how to cope with it.* New York: Seabury, 1977. This book is primarily addressed to older children and adolescents, but it can also be read with profit by adults. The author's purpose is to help readers achieve a

better understanding of the impact of loss and of the
normality of responses that may at first seem unusual. In
addition to practical guidance, there is information on
books, films, and organizational resources that are relevant
to this subject.

Bluebond-Langner, M. *The private worlds of dying children.*
Princeton, N.J.: Princeton University Press, 1978. What
distinguishes this book is the effort by its author to examine
the distinctive worlds of dying children from the viewpoint
of a cultural anthropologist. The children in question ranged
in age from three to nine years old. They all had leukemia
and were observed during the author's research in the
pediatric ward of a large teaching hospital. Many adults
believe that small children are unaware of their condition;
previous research and this study contradict such wishful
thinking. Hence, the key issues here are: How do these
children come to know that they are dying when no one
tells them (a process of socialization), and how or why do
they choose to conceal this awareness from adults (a reflection of the social order that they have accepted)? These
issues are exemplified in a playlet that dramatizes the world
of a composite dying child, which is then subjected to
careful theoretical analysis. The author's conclusions challenge common viewpoints and the methodologies of many
earlier studies; her book can be read with profit by most
adults but is indispensable for those who work with or seek
to understand dying children. A short appendix discusses
problems involved in doing this sort of field work.

Claypool, J. *Tracks of a fellow struggler: How to handle grief.*
Waco, Tex.: Word, 1974. John Claypool is a Baptist minister
who experienced the death of his eight-year-old daughter,
Laura Lue. This short book consists of four sermons in
which Claypool shared his experiences with his congrega-
tions. The sermons were preached on the occasion of the
diagnosis of acute leukemia, nine months later at the end of
the first remission, four weeks after Laura Lue died, and one
year afterward. The perspective is that of biblical Christianity, but it is also very personal and human. The book
conveys suffering, strong feelings, and questioning, together
with a sense of survival, healing, and growth.

Fargues, M. *The child and the mystery of death* (Sister Gertrude, S. P., Trans.). Glen Rock, N.J.: Paulist, 1966. Marie Fargues is a prominent figure in the French Catholic catechetical movement. In this slim paperback English version of her book, she combines religious and psychological perspectives to guide the pastoral teaching of children about death. The book is divided into three principal parts representing, respectively, the points of view of observers, families, and pedagogy. Each of these sections conclude with 15 study-club questions for discussion.

Fassler, J. *Helping children cope* (W. B. Hogan, Illus.). New York: Free Press, 1978. A reference guide by an author and student of children's literature. The book addresses stress that might be brought about by death, separation experiences, hospitalization and illness, lifestyle changes, and events or situations. In each case the author joins a brief discussion of professional viewpoints on the topic to an analysis of selected books (mainly for four- to eight-year-olds) that might help children deal with stress. For example, the 25-page section on death provides a narrative account of strong and weak points in some 30 books ranging from stories about change or death in nature, pets, and humans to informational books and books about the death of a child. Thoughtful, but far more limited than the Bernstein volume.

Furman, E. (Ed.). *A child's parent dies: Studies in childhood bereavement.* New Haven, Conn.: Yale University Press, 1974. The classic volume on bereavement in childhood from a psychoanalytic viewpoint. The editor provides here, on behalf of her colleagues, an introductory account of the study on which this book is based, theoretical insights on helping bereaved children, grief and mourning, the process of mourning, individual circumstances, differences between children and adults in mourning, effects of parental death on the child's personality development, and observations on depression and apathy, and a 64-page review of literature that relates this work to other studies. Meanwhile, nine lengthy examples by individual therapists appear throughout the text. Indispensable for professionals.

Gordon, A. K., & Klass, D. *They need to know: How to teach children about death.* Englewood Cliffs, N.J.: Prentice-Hall,

1979. Intended primarily for parents and teachers, this book marks an important advance over earlier, less sophisticated works on death education for children. Part I offers a background sketch of the interaction between children, adults, and death in our society, and general guidelines for parents and teachers. Part II outlines a program for death education including four overall goals, suggested curricula with specific resources and activities by grade and goal, and consumer information regarding medical and funeral services. Nine appendixes reproduce documents like a living will, natural death legislation, and a patient's bill of rights that are useful in this kind of education. Readers will particularly benefit from the pedagogical schema provided by Gordon and Klass, which they can now supplement from our more extensive list of resources.

Green, B. R., & Irish, D. P. *Death education: Preparation for living.* Cambridge, Mass.: Schenkman, 1971. This slim paperback of less than 150 pages is based on a symposium held at Hamline University, St. Paul, Minnesota, in February 1970. Three invited speakers included: Herman Feifel, who surveys the meaning of death in American society; John Brantner, who reflects on implications of death for the self; and Daniel Leviton, who discusses the role of the schools in providing death education. Following the texts of these three major addresses is an essay by Donald P. Irish, who argues from a sociological viewpoint that death education at various levels can properly be seen as preparation for living. Finally, there are excerpts from 12 discussion groups at the symposium and a selected bibliography. Now 10 years old, but still of interest and value.

Grollman, E. A. (Ed.), *Explaining death to children.* Boston: Beacon, 1967. Grollman is a well-known rabbi, counselor, and writer in the field of separation and loss, and his book is a pioneering effort to help adults deal with children and death. Now dated and limited in several ways, *Explaining death to children* still contains some interesting chapters: Robert Fulton on death in our society, Gregory Rochlin on strong feelings that very young children seem to have about death, Robert Kastenbaum on the development of children's understanding of death, and an unusual piece by Claiborne Jones on biologic aspects of death. There are also chapters on Protestant, Catholic, and Jewish perspectives on death, and an early essay on children's literature. The author of this last piece maintains that for the young child up to about age eight "there is little need in his spring-green world for an understanding of the dead" (p. 250), a contention with which many experts disagree.

Grollman, E. A. *Talking about death: A dialogue between parent and child* (G. Héau, Illus.). Boston: Beacon, 1976. This book is described as "a new edition with a Parent's Guide and recommended resources" of the 1970 book by the same title. It begins with a 25-page section of text and pictures that is meant to be read along with young children. The parent's guide then responds to typical questions, statements, or situations that might come up in connection with this joint reading experience. Here the author stresses the need to combine straightforward honesty with sensitive support. Two concluding sections describe recommended individuals, organizations, books, and audiovisuals from which additional information and assistance can be obtained. This is probably the best-known resource in the field for parents of young children.

Gunther, J. *Death be not proud: A memoir.* New York: Harper, 1949. Johnny Gunther died in 1947 at the age of 17; this book is his father's story of Johnny's fight for life in the 14 months before his death. *Death be not proud* is very well known for many reasons: It is an early example of its type; its author is a prominent writer; and it has recently been made into a film for television. The story is one of a gallant and brilliant young man, a malignant brain tumor, frantic efforts at orthodox and heterodox treatment, tension with phsyicans, and both good and bad times before death. A concluding section contains some of Johnny's letters, extracts from his diary, and a haunting afterword by his mother.

Gyulay, J. E. *The dying child.* New York: McGraw-Hill, 1978. This book is aimed primarily at members of the health care team; its author is a pediatric nurse. Four central parts discuss: concerns of the child—young children, older children, and special children, such as those who are physically or emotionally handicapped, mentally retarded, adopted, from one-parent families, of foreign descent, twins, or an only child; problems affecting the grievers—parents, siblings, and significant others (taken very broadly); phases of illness and death, from diagnosis through remission, relapse, the terminal state, or sudden loss, to the postdeath period; and guidelines for nursing care of dying children. No references within the text, but an extensive bibliography at the end. Commendable for its broad scope. Otherwise not particularly new but useful as a blend of existing knowledge and common-sense insights.

Hughes, P. R. *Dying is different.* Mahomet, Ill.: Mech Mentor Education, 1978. The author has designed this book to promote discussion of death between adults and preschool through second-grade children. The 18 children's pages use drawings, strong colors, and poems to present a graduated succession of living and dead states in flowers, ants, fish, a cat, and a grandmother, followed by vivid thematic depictions of the inevitability of death, its justification, remembering, acceptance, grief, funerals, cemeteries, and the importance of love during life. An introduction, facing pages for adults, and some concluding remarks suggest questions and guidelines for parents and teachers. The book can be read alone either by children or by adults, but it is perhaps best used jointly as a basis for sharing. Available in both a large instructional edition designed to stand upright by itself and a smaller personal edition in standard book form.

Irish, J. A. *A boy thirteen: Reflections on death.* Philadelphia: Westminster, 1975. In 1973 the Irish family (parents and two sons; a third, younger son had died in 1969 of a congenital heart defect) was accompanying a student group in Europe when their 13-year-old son suddenly died of acute meningitis. The boy's father—a teacher of philosophy and theology—wrote this short essay, as he says, in an effort "to articulate my own response to Lee's incomprehensible death" (p. 18). It explores anger at the unacceptability of death, aloneness and the abandonment of death, and freedom in the opportunity to love and thereby to overcome ending and separation.

Jackson, E. N. *Telling a child about death.* New York: Hawthorn, 1965. From a Protestant minister and counselor who has written extensively on grief, stress, funerals, and children, 83 pages of practical advice. Jackson's basic premise is that "the emotional crises of life can be used to teach wise response to deprivation and loss" (p. 23). Thus, *both* children and adults can benefit from sharing ideas and feelings that are related to death.

Klagsbrun, F. *Too young to die: Youth and suicide.* Boston: Houghton Mifflin, 1976; New York: Pocket Books, 1977. This is the first book about suicide among adolescents and college students that was written to be read by young people as well as by their parents, counselors, and teachers. Its three parts deal, respectively, with: the realities of suicide among the young, that is, statistics, common myths, suicide as a communication, the role of depression or psychosis, and uncounted or "chronic" suicides; practical guidelines—What can you do?—for dealing both with crisis situations and with survivors; and social aspects, that is, sociological or psychological causes, cultural attitudes, and prevention techniques. Appendixes document the sharp rise in suicide rates among the 15- to 24-year-old age group over the 20-year period from 1954 to 1974 and list many suicide prevention or crisis intervention agencies in the United States. There is also an eight-page bibliography. A good introduction for adults to an increasingly important subject.

Kotzwinkle, W. *Swimmer in the secret sea.* New York: Avon, 1975. This is a deeply moving account of a young couple's joyful preparation for the birth of their child (the figure in the title), sudden complications during the birth process, unsuccessful attempts of the medical personnel to bring their stillborn son back to life, and their decision to build a simple pine box and bury their baby in the woods. Descriptions are grimly realistic, and the language is taut and powerful. The reader is not protected from the shock and pain experienced by the parents. Some readers may even be appalled at times by the stark and unmitigated reality of the descriptions. For example, when the parents receive their dead baby in a green plastic garbage bag after having consented to an autopsy and open the bag, they find that the little boy had not been sewed together again. Despite such almost unspeakable experiences, the young couple comes to accept the death of their son. The message is one of triumph of love and faith. This short story is a must.

Langone, J. *Death is a noun: A view of the end of life.* Boston: Little, Brown, 1972; New York: Dell, 1975. John Langone is a medical journalist who surveys here many prominent social issues concerning death. Using research reports, historical analyses, and human interest stories, he deals with basic attitudes toward death, with euthanasia, abortion, capital punishment, murder, suicide, the problem of determining the presence of death, grief, and the mystery of death. Langone writes clearly and simply for young readers, but his book can also serve as the simplest introduction to the field of death and dying for adults.

Langone, J. *Vital signs: The way we die in America.* Boston: Little, Brown, 1974. This book is a kind of documentary drama, "a work of assembly," as the author terms it. Focusing on dying, Langone skillfully weaves together a variety of materials: classical quotations, scientific data, legal case material, news reports, and interviews conducted with doctors, nurses, clergy, and dying people and their families. The themes are communication and caring, those giving and those receiving. As he informs, Langone also calls us to greater empathy for the needs of dying people. Another good place for mature young readers and adults to begin their inquiry.

LeShan, E. *Learning to say good-by: When a parent dies* (P. -Giovanopoulos, Illus.). New York: Macmillan, 1978. Eda LeShan is a well-known writer and family counselor who speaks here to children in a simple, straightforward manner about the problems they face when losing a parent and how to overcome them. The main thrust throughout this helpful and comforting book is the acceptance of the griever as a person who is suffering much pain and disorientation but who is healthy and will be capable of coping by expressing and sharing her or his feelings in open communication with interested and caring adults. The book is well written, and examples are used liberally to illustrate a situation or clarify a point. An informative, nonthreatening, supportive book that can be quite useful for sympathetic and concerned adults.

Lonetto, R. *Children's conceptions of death.* New York: Springer, 1980. This is the most detailed, recent effort to understand the development of children's views of death. The investigation is framed in the context of our general knowledge of childhood development and in the light of previous research on death-related concepts. But the special feature of this book is its extensive interviews with Canadian children as reflected in the reproduction of many of their comments and drawings. This research suggests three general phases in the development of children's concepts of death from ages 3 through 12. A concluding chapter briefly considers special problems of dying children, childhood bereavement, and explaining death to a child.

Lund, E. *Eric.* Philadelphia: Lippincott, 1974. In 1967 just before he was about to go off to college, Doris Lund's 17-year-old son was found to have acute lymphocytic leukemia. This book is about the 4 1/2 years that followed until his death. During that time, Eric went in and out of remission as he endured the twin hardships of disease and chemotherapy. Always he fought hungrily to experience life, insisting on running his own risks and living his own life. Eric obliged his parents to give him the freedom to be himself, a difficult task under normal circumstances and one made ever more demanding under the shadow of life-threatening illness. *Eric* combines candor, courage, wit, and sadness in a compelling way without ever descending into sentimentality and self-pity.

Mills, G. C., Reisler, R., Robinson, A. E., & Vermilye, G. *Discussing death: A guide to death education.* Homewood, Ill.: ETC, 1976. This curriculum guide for educators is divided into four age levels: 5-6 years, 7-9 years, 10-12, years, and 13-18 years. Within each level, it describes curricular concepts and a series of learning opportunities (e.g., life cycles or grief expression) and suggests specific objectives, activities, and resources or strategies for teachers. Flawed, oversimplified, and now superceded by better and more reliable guides.

Reed, E. L. *Helping children with the mystery of death.* Nasvhille, Tenn.: Abingdon, 1970. Offered as "a book of religious substance," about half of the space in this volume is given to resources for adults and children, such as biblical and poetic excerpts, stories, suggested activities, and prayers. The text shares this concern for Christian education.

Roach, N. *The last day of April.* New York: American Cancer Society, 1974. This little 40-page booklet tells a mother's story of the time between her 2 1/2-year-old daughter's diagnosis of leukemia and Erin's death 4 1/2 years later. The twin principles that guided these parents came to them early, after two months of grief and self-pity: "We had to stop feeling sorry for ourselves," and "hard as it would be to lose her someday, it would be easier knowing we had done all we could for her." A powerful tale sharing simple lessons learned at great price.

Rudolph, M. *Should the children know? Encounters with death in the lives of children.* New York: Schocken, 1978. When 4 1/2-year-old Rachel died suddenly at home, the author called an urgent parents' meeting to ask what she should tell the children in her nursery school class. Although the parents were unsure what to do, it became evident that the children wanted to be told the truth about their classmate (whether they understood it fully or not), and they wanted to be given an opportunity to share the thoughts and feelings engendered by this event. In this book, the author argues for such honesty and sharing and suggests ways to help preschool children deal with death through books, caring for plants and animals, and direct experience with human death.

Sahler, O. J. (Ed.). *The child and death.* St. Louis: Mosby, 1978. Growing out of a 1977 symposium at the University of Rochester Medical Center, this book consists of 23 papers by professionals on the following general subjects: families and the death or fatal illness of a child, with some principles for helping; viewpoints and problems of those who care for dying or chronically ill children; survivors—of death or suicide, whether they be children, parents, or grandparents, and how some might be helped by bereavement parents' groups; and ethical or educational considerations, including issues for the clergy, the right to information and freedom of choice for dying minors, a program for death education at the high school level, and an annotated bibliography categorized by a modified Kübler-Ross schema. The book opens with a short preface and introduction by the editor and a chapter on the development of the child's concept of death; it closes with two short personal statements by the mother and sister of a child who died at three months of age. Many good chapters for professionals, with some fuzziness in conception and unevenness in execution.

Smith, A. A. *Rachel.* Wilton, Conn.: Morehouse-Barlow, 1974. The author is an Episcopal priest who experienced the sudden and unexpected death of one of his daughters when she was 10 years old. In this 55-page booklet, he describes the impact of that event on himself and his family in order to share with others in similar situations a sense of normalcy in the midst of the abnormal. Short lists of things for surviving parents to do or not to do and gentle advice for outsiders manage to be practical and helpful without becoming preachy. The concluding paragraph summarizes an orientation for everyone:

> Death is not a private affair. Except for rare instances, every death affects many people in varying ways. The entire community is, or should be, involved in helping those affected most to resume a normal life. This should never take the form of trying to erase the memories or the hurt, rather it should enable those hurt most to accept death as a normal, inevitable, and necessary part of our humanity. (p. 55)

Stanford, G., & Perry, D. *Death out of the closet: A cirriculum guide to living with dying.* New York: Bantam, 1976. This fairly early book in the field is addressed mainly to teachers and counselors. It offers a rationale for death education at the secondary school level and suggestions regarding problems (with principals, parents, students, or lack of prior training) that such programs are likely to encounter. Beyond that, the authors propose topics, materials, and strategies for introducing different aspects of death education in various curricular contexts. The last chapter of the book (occupying nearly half of its 200-odd pages) provides questions for study or discussion and synopses of 19 books (mainly by the same publisher) that seem to be popular or particularly suited for young people. There are some good things here but also fairly obvious defects and limitations. Critical users can benefit from Stanford and Perry, but most will appreciate the greater sophistication and expertise of Gordon and Klass.

Sternberg, F., & Sternberg, B. *If I die and when I do: Exploring death with young people.* Englewood Cliffs, N.J.: Prentice-Hall, 1980. Based on the experiences of a junior high school social studies teacher who accidentally stumbled into teaching a nine-week death and dying class, the bulk of this book is the work of children themselves. The narrative text describes the organization of the course and lays out a skeleton structure of key topics, such as sharing experiences about death; exploring beliefs; dealing with fears, humor, old age; and facing our own deaths. But the most lengthy and interesting parts of the book are the many interspersed statements, poems, and drawings by the students.

Talking to children about death (U.S. Department of Health, Education, and Welfare Publication No. (ADM)79-838), Washington, 1979. Single free copies are available by writing to: Public Inquiries, National Institute of Mental Health, 5600 Fishers Lane, Rockville, MD 20857. This short pamphlet from the federal government surveys issues of death-related communications with children and recommends sensible approaches to common problems or situations. The briefest introduction that could be recommended.

Ulin, R. O. *Death and dying education.* Washington: National Education Association, 1977. Ulin argues the appropriateness in the schools of death education that is designed "to expose young people in an unthreatening way to some of the facts about death, aging, and dying in our society, to introduce them to a variety of perspectives from other cultures and from artists, philosophers, sociologists, psychologists, poets, and novelists, and most importantly, to help them sort out their own thinking on the subject" (p. 40). He also discusses preparations and qualifications for teachers in the field and includes an outline of a high school course on death and dying. There is a short bibliography and list of audiovisual resources. One can find better curriculum and resource guides, but the detailed rationale for death education and the sponsorship of this book make it useful.

Vogel, L. J. *Helping a child understand death.* Philadelphia: Fortress, 1975. Linda Jane Vogel teaches Christian education at a college in Iowa. This thin paperback book is intended to offer guidance for those who share her religious convictions. It is based on her personal experiences and some not-very-sophisticated reading in the field of death and dying. Elementary but quite readable.

Wass, H. (Ed.). *Dying: Facing the facts.* Washington: Hemisphere, 1979. This is one of the best and most recent comprehensive basic texts on death and dying. It is used in many college classrooms and can be read with profit by professional people and other interested parties. Nearly all of the material in this book has been newly written by experts in their respective fields. Topics covered include: death in our society, physiology and psychosocial aspects of dying, dying in institutions, hospice programs, the elderly, funeral practices, bereavement and grief, the law, defining death, euthanasia, and death education. A chapter on children and death should be of special interest to the readers of this volume. It provides a concise review of research and clinical studies dealing with children's death concepts, anxieties, and grief reactions and offers suggestions for parents and professionals on how to help effectively. Provides a broad basic background.

Wass, H., & Corr, C. A. (Eds.). *Childhood and death.* Washington: Hemisphere, in press. This will be a valuable reference work for medical personnel, counseling practitioners, clergy, teachers, and parents as well as a major textbook for the student in the health and helping professions. All chapters in this book present newly written material by experts in the respective specializations. Some of the topics have not been discussed in any book before. Topics covered include: patterns of coping in dying children; the pediatrician's role; how other care givers can help; helping parents, siblings, and health professionals cope with a dying child; children's patterns of mourning; stillbirth, neonatal death, sudden infant death syndrome and how to help survivors grieve; suicide in childhood; the development of death concepts and anxieties; and death education in home and school. Highly recommended.

Wass, H., Corr, C. A., Pacholski, R. A., & Sanders, C. M. *Death education: An annotated resource guide.* Washington: Hemisphere, 1980. A comprehensive, annotated resource guide intended primarily for those who teach in this area, but many sections will be valuable for others. Coverage includes: printed resources—books and articles describing death education for all levels and audiences, selected text and reference books, bibliographies, periodicals, and literature on research and assessment of death attitudes; audiovisual resources—films, videotapes, filmstrips, slides, audio tapes, and cassettes, together with distributors; organizational resources; community resources; and an appendix with last-minute entries. An indispensable reference tool.

Watts, R. G. *Straight talk about death with young people.* Philadelphia: Westminster, 1975. Based on discussion groups with junior high school students, this short paperback by a Presbyterian minister is intended to illustrate the kinds of issues and approaches that interest such students. The central topics are learning about death, dying, grief, funerals, and beliefs about life after death. Useful in the context from which it originated.

White, J. D. *Talking with a child* (J. Orlando, Illus.). New York: Macmillan, 1976. This book "is intended to help adults to have a pleasant, positive time sharing language" (p. x) with children. A bright and interesting account of a wide range of elements in successful interactions with children. The chapter on death (pp. 229–252) might be read on its own by those who do not have time for anything longer.

Wolf, A. W. M. *Helping your child to understand death*. New York: Child Study, 1958; rev. ed., 1973. A very successful book of advice and counsel by a child development specialist writing for parents and other concerned adults. The text of approximately 60 pages consists of some prefatory material, a short three-page introduction to the setting and aims of the book, two long chapters addressed respectively to issues posed by children and those raised by parents, and a brief conclusion on our religious and cultural heritages in regard to death. The twin central chapters are organized around typical questions or statements used as focuses for analysis and discussion. The advice that emerges takes shape as a sensible and constructive program for familial and other interactions with children about death.

Zeligs, R. *Children's experience with death*. Springfield, Ill.: Thomas, 1974. Written by a child psychologist, this book attempts a very broad reach in both scope and audience. For the latter, it intends to be useful for readers ranging from high school students and parents to professionals such as clergy persons, nurses, social workers, and physicians. For the former, it discusses developmental concepts and fears of death, sick and dying children, the handicapped child, suicide, parental death, and religion. Simply written for those who seek a broad overview, but there are better books now available on most of these subjects.

∞∞

BOOKS FOR CHILDREN
AN ANNOTATED BIBLIOGRAPHY

∞∞

HANNELORE WASS

In the 18th and 19th centuries, children's books were written primarily by clergymen or their wives or daughters. "Death," "hell," and "judgment" were part of almost all stories and were often portrayed in a frightening manner to teach the child moral behavior. At the end of the 19th century religious leaders departed from the grim stance of traditional dogma to a liberal position in which "hell" and "damnation" were replaced by the comforting concept that death means "going to Heaven" and "God's call to come home to eternal bliss." Then, too, with the development of public education late in the 19th century, the role of the church in the education of children diminished. Correspondingly, there was less emphasis on death in children's books. Decreasing infant mortality further reinforced this trend, and death almost disappeared from children's literature except from books of rhymes, fairy tales, and the McGuffey Readers series published as children's reading texts from 1836 to 1936 and used primarily in the schools of the midwest.

The 20th century is in many ways the "century of the child" in which individuals and society beyond the bounds of churches and synagogues are concerned with the development of values and the use of constructive and benign means to help children grow into maturity. Among the many demonstrations of these concerns is an extensive literature specifically written for children and adolescents by writers who are sensitive to the needs of the young and who possess deep insights into their world of perceptions, thoughts, and feelings. In most of the books written by such writers early in this century and in many recent volumes, the subject of death is embedded in the main theme and not specifically emphasized. Many of these books are outstanding. They depict death as a significant part of life within a variety of themes. Examples of classics of this kind are M. K. Rawling's *The Yearling,* E. B. White's *Charlotte's Web,* and P. S. Buck's *The Big Wave.* Among the recent books of this kind are M. L'Engle's *A Ring of Endless Light,* B. Miles's *The Trouble with Thirteen,* and P. R. Naylor's *To Walk the Sky Path.*

In recent years a new death awareness in our society has stimulated a desire to cope more effectively with dying and death and to help others do so. Probably inspired by this Zeitgeist, a new genre of gifted writers has chosen death as the main theme of their stories, both fictional and nonfictional. J. Fassler's *My Grandpa Died Today,* P. R. Hughes's *Dying is Different,* D. B. Smith's *A Taste of Blackberries,* A. Slote's *Hang Tough, Paul Mather,* H. Zim's and S. Bleeker's *Life and Death* are but a few of the many moving and inspiring books available today. All books that deal well with death can be helpful, but those that *center* on the subject require special sensitivity and can be particularly informative and therapeutic, not only for children but for adults as well.

This bibliography was begun modestly with a listing of 25 books first published in *Childhood Education* and in the chapter "Children and Death" in H. Wass (Ed.),*Dying: Facing the facts,* Washington, Hemisphere, 1979, and has grown to a total of 156 titles. The selection of books was guided by my judgment that the portrayal of dying, death, and grief in a book is sensitive and realistic, low-keyed rather than sensational or melodramatic, honest and straightforward rather than vague or evasive, and believable rather than exotic, all in the general context of hope and the strength of the human spirit. I have attempted to provide a good balance of books for various age groups, but there are relatively few books available for the very young child, and this is reflected in the bibliography. Obviously, I missed some oustanding books because they did not come to my attention or, in some cases, were simply not obtainable. I do think, however, that the titles listed below are representative of the field.

Aaron, C. *Catch Calico!* New York: Dutton, 1979. Fiction. Age 12 and over. Fourteen-year-old Louis goes with his grandfather to the mountain cabin to catch Calico, a semiwild cat who has lived near the cabin for 10 years, is getting old and blind, and is not likely to survive the harsh mountain winter that is fast approaching. Grandfather explains that it will be better to shoot Calico than to leave her to die slowly and in misery. But Calico scratches and bites Grandfather, who soon afterward gets very sick. Being the son of a doctor, Grandfather realizes that Calico is rabid, but he cannot get his shots in time. The story tells about how Louis copes with his grandfather's worsening condition and his eventual death, how Louis learns to gather the courage to shoot Calico himself, and how he mourns both losses. A highly readable story of love, pain, courage, and strength of spirit.

Abbot, S. *The old dog.* (G. Mocniak, illus.). New York: Coward, 1972. Fiction. Ages 8-10. Ben's old dog dies in her sleep one night and leaves her young owner lonely and bereft when he realizes that his pet is not only asleep but will never again play and run with him and lick his hands and face. The technique of shadow illustrations to depict Ben's memories is very effective. Whereas silhouettes are used to portray memories, orange is used to portray current reality. A shortcoming of this story is that Ben's parents do not allow him time to grieve his dead pet. His father brings home a new puppy the same evening, implying that loved ones are interchangeable. Otherwise good.

Agee, J. *A death in the family.* New York: Avon, 1938. Fiction. Age 14 and over. This Pulitzer Prize-winning novel is a classic. It vividly portrays the wide range of emotions that are evoked in the members of a family by the death of one of them. This is a powerful saga of human strengths and weaknesses in the face of tragedy. The author has great depth of insight into the complex world and emotions of a growing child and his or her attempt to make sense out of the events in which he or she participates and to understand those who love and care for him or her.

Alcott, L. M. *Little women.* Boston: Little, Brown, 1968. Fiction. Ages 9-13. This popular piece of fiction provides a wholesome introduction to, and a vicarious experience of, the inevitability of death and the grief it causes. Beth, one

of the four March sisters, dies surrounded by her loving
family. This closely knit Civil War–era New England family
grieve for their beloved Beth, but the young reader is left
with the impression that the grieving is made easier by the
sharing and the strength of the family bond. A very skillful
portrayal of the pain of mourning and the continuity of life
and interpersonal relationships.

Anckarsvärd, K. *Springtime for Eva* (A. Macmillan, Trans., from
Swedish). New York: Harcourt, 1959. Fiction. Age 12 and
over. This novel sensitively explores a young girl's attitude
toward death and her relationships with family and friends.
Eva tries and succeeds in putting the death of her friend in
perspective, in accepting the fact that life must go on. This
healthy understanding of death is contrasted to Lena's
morbid brooding, for Lena chooses to dwell on death so that
she can elicit sympathy for herself.

Angell, J. *Ronnie and Rosey.* Scarsdale, N.Y.: Bradbury, 1977.
Fiction. Ages 12-14. After 13-year-old Ronnie Rachman and
her parents move to Uniondale and a new junior high school
on Long Island, it takes some time for her to meet and
make new friends. Just when she has formed a threesome
with Evelyn Racanelli and Robert Rose, Ronnie's father is
killed in an automobile accident. Ronnie and her mother
deal with their grief first by clinging to each other and later
by withdrawing, each into herself. They attempt to cope
with their pain by repressing thoughts and feelings about
their dead father and husband. Their growing estrangement is
compounded as Ronnie and Robert begin meeting each other
secretly without their parents' permission in order to share
each other's company. Ronnie and her mother have different
needs during this difficult time, which they only realize after
a major confrontation. Finally, they both see that they must
allow each other independence in order to go forward
together.

Armstrong, W. *Sounder.* New York: Harper, 1969. Fiction. Age 11
and over. After stealing a ham to feed his family, a black
sharecropper is taken away to jail. In the process, Sounder,
the family dog, is shot at and runs off. The sharecropper's
son is happy when Sounder comes hobbling back home.

When the father is transferred to a labor camp, the boy sets out to search for his father. A kind schoolmaster takes him into his home, where he does chores and attends school. During one of the boy's visits home, he finds his father has returned but is ill and dies. A gripping story of hardship, stoic suffering in the face of death, resilience, and self-reliance.

Arundel, H. *The blanket word.* Nashville, Tenn.: Nelson, 1973. Fiction. Age 15 and over. The blanket word is *love,* which for Janette Meredith, the brilliant 19-year-old student, means family responsibility. Jan is the youngest of four children. Her two sisters and her brother are all married, have families, and are all dutiful family people. Jan does not care for her family, and she is honest about it. But news that her mother is dying of cancer produces in Jan an emotional turmoil for which she is unprepared. On the train returning home she is filled with guilt and self-reproach for having missed vacations at home, for not having called, having failed to write letters, and not having done thoughtful things for her mother. Her feelings turn to rage when she discovers that her sisters and brother had failed to tell her of her mother's illness until her mother was in the final difficult and painful phase of dying. Jan hates Mrs. Williams, the nurse, who reports that her mother is making "splendid progress." This hypocrisy—in fact, any kind of hypocrisy—is appalling to Jan. This includes some of the conventions of the funeral arrangements. Eventually, back in college, Jan discovers her admiration for her brother Jim, who with quiet efficiency and deep care has taken responsibility and has helped the family during her mother's final day and following her death. Jan learns that she loves her brother and is ready to help when he needs her. This well-written, thought-provoking book sensitively portrays young people's idealism and self-doubts. Its most striking feature is the insistence on honesty in matters of filial and familial love even in the face of death.

Asinoff, E. *Craig and Joan: Two lives for peace.* New York: Viking, 1971. Nonfiction. Age 14 and over. Two teen-agers, Craig and Joan, products of a conservative upbringing, form a suicide pact and commit suicide to protest the Vietnam

War. The author's interviews of Craig's and Joan's relatives and friends form the major portion of the book. Why do two well-liked adolescents elect to die to speak out against war? Is altruistic suicide an "appropriate" and defensible means of protest? Are there better alternatives? This book forces the reader to confront basic issues of war, destruction, self-destruction, and idealism. It is recommended as reading to be followed by group discussion or dialogue with parents.

Babbitt, N. *The eyes of the Amaryllis.* New York: Farrar, 1977. Fiction. Ages 9–11. In 1880, thirty years after the sinking of the brig *Amaryllis,* Geneva Reade still waits in her ocean-side house for a message from her dead husband, the ship's captain. When Geneva's granddaughter, Jenny, comes for a visit, she too is drawn into the twice-daily searches at high tide for the communication. She meets a strange person on the beach who is said to be the man who had carved the figurehead for the *Amaryllis* and later attempted suicide on the spot where the ship had sunk. One day the sea gives up a sign—the figurehead—but the man urges Geneva and Jenny to give it back; when they refuse, the sea rises in a fierce hurricane and reclaims the figurehead. An adventure of the sea, rich in fantasy and imagination.

Bartoli, J. *Nonna.* New York: Harvey House, 1975. Fiction. Preschool to 7. This story is about a young boy who learns to accept the death of his grandmother Nonna. At first he refuses to believe that Nonna is gone and he can no longer get cookies and gifts from her and that she will never play with him again. Eventually new people move into Nonna's house and life goes on. But the memories of the boy's grandmother are cherished. The story portrays the need for patience and the need for understanding that young children may respond to the death of a loved one in very specific and concrete ways.

Bauer, M. D. *Shelter from the wind.* New York: Seabury, 1976. Fiction. Ages 10–14. Twelve-year-old Stacy resents her step-mother, Barbara, especially since Barbara is pregnant. So one day in a blind rage, Stacy runs away from home. After long, hot hours of walking in the desert, Stacy comes upon two German shepherds who guide her to the little stone house where an old woman, Ella, lives as a recluse. Through helping take care of a litter of puppies, having to see one sick puppy mercifully killed by Ella, and through absorbing Ella's philosophy of life, Stacy comes to grips with her own problems and decides to return home and try to get along with Barbara. The plot is loosely woven, but the story is well told.

Bawden, N. M. K. *Squib*. Philadelphia: Lippincott, 1971. Fiction. Ages 11–13. Twelve-year-old Kate Pollack has difficulty facing the reality of death. Her father has drowned after saving Kate and unsuccessfully trying to save her little brother, Rupert. Later, playing with her friends in the park, Kate sees a strange, frail, shy little boy called Squib and soon convinces herself that he is her little brother, who had somehow survived. The children discover that Squib is mistreated by his guardian and report this to their families. Squib is then removed legally from the care of his guardian. Kate is now forced to accept her young brother's death and Squib's true identity.

Bernstein, J. E. *Loss and how to cope with it*. New York: Seabury, 1977. Nonfiction. Age 12 and over. In this book the author addresses older children and adolescents and discusses in a straightforward manner the responses of people to the death of a loved one, stressing that many reactions that are apparently bizarre are actually normal and common. The author relates personal stories that serve effectively to make a point or convey a concept. Along the way, much practical advice is offered to the reader. The book includes a list of other books on death and dying as well as some films and organizational resources. Valuable not only for children and youth, but for adults as well.

Bernstein, J. E., & Gullo, S. V. *When people die* (R. Hausherr, Photographer). New York: Dutton, 1977. Nonfiction. Ages 6–10. This sensitive, beautifully written book explains honestly and at the same time reassuringly how people feel and act when a loved one dies and gently leads the reader through the grieving process, including shock and denial; physical distress; and feelings of emptiness, anger, and isolation. The authors do not shy away from dealing with the biologic and physiological aspects of death, decomposition, and body disposal. This book answers many questions children ask about death. The stunningly beautiful photographs by the young Swiss photographer add greatly to the value of the book. Particularly striking and poignant are the photos of the newborn infant who has just entered the world and whose wrinkled face expresses need for care, followed a page later by the beautiful face of an old woman (actually Mrs. Michaelson, a retired principal) whose wrinkles tell of the joys and sorrows of a long life well-lived and of wisdom and serenity achieved. A must.

Bluenose, P., & Carpenter, W. S. *Two knots on a counting rope* (J. Smith, Illus.). New York: Holt, 1964. Fiction. Ages 6–9. This simply told story centers around a young Navajo Indian boy's respect and love for his grandfather, who teaches him many things. Among them, he teaches the boy how to count, using knots in a rope. The rope and its knots are symbolic of a person's life. After the last knot, one dies. Life and death are connected. Death is a natural part of the life cycle.

Borack, B. *Someone small* (A. Lobel, Illus.). New York: Harper, 1969. Fiction. Preschool to age 7. This story describes a young girl's gradual acceptance of her new sister and her love for her pet bird, Fluffy. One day Fluffy dies. The girls wrap him in a handkerchief, kiss him good-by, put him in a box, say a prayer, and bury him, thus going through a full funeral ritual. The colored pictures are essential to the story, for they portray feelings not specifically mentioned in the text.

Bradbury, B. *Where's Jim now?* Boston: Houghton Mifflin, 1978. Fiction. Ages 12–16. The difficulties experienced by a woman, Beth, and her 15-year-old son, David, after the death of her husband are complicated by the sudden reappearance of a troubled older son, Jim, from the father's first marriage. Beth and David try to take in the older boy, but the relationship never quite works out and Jim is eventually killed by a prison buddy. Divorce and death often have tragic consequences for those left behind. This story is starkly realistic.

Bradley, B. *Endings: A book about death.* Reading, Mass.: Addison-Wesley, 1979. Nonfiction. Ages 12–14. This book for young people ranges across the field of death and dying in order to provoke discussion and reflection. The author is a professional writer, not a content expert. Nevertheless, his information is up-to-date, and individual discussions are clear, even though it is sometimes difficult to follow the order of the chapters and their internal subdivisions. The text makes good use of model cases and literary references to illustrate points.

Brooks, J. *Uncle Mike's boy.* New York: Harper, 1973. Fiction. Age 9 and over. Pudge is a lonely boy whose only friend, his younger sister, has died as a result of a car accident, which Pudge himself survived. His parents offer no comfort because they cannot deal with their own problems. Fortunately, the boy's Uncle Mike, who himself has suffered the loss of two loved ones, offers Pudge support and friendship. With Uncle Mike's help, Pudge regains his self-confidence and is able to cope with his grief and the guilt he feels over his sister's death and his own survival. With his uncle's help, he is also able to cope with his mother's remarriage and his father's mental breakdown. A story of a grim reality, unsentimental but believable. Sometimes it is not the parents but a relative who provides the nurture needed to cope with hardships.

Brown, M. W. *The dead bird.* Reading, Mass.: Addison-Wesley, 1965. Fiction. Preschool to age 8. A group of children find a dead bird in the park. They observe what "dead" is like by touching and looking. Then they decide to have a funeral and bury the bird before resuming their play. Each day the children return to the bird's grave, put fresh flowers on it, and sing to the bird. They continue this ritual of mourning "until they forg[e]t." The final illustration depicts the children as they play ball, with the bird's grave in the background. The author's insight and understanding of young children is evident. The story is straightforward, practical, detailed, and matter-of-fact, yet tender and caring. Valuable.

Buck, P. S. *The big wave.* New York: Scholastic, 1960. Fiction. Ages 9–11. Pearl Buck's classic tale of Jiya, the fisherman's son, whose family is killed by a tidal wave and who then goes to live with his friend Kino, the farmer's son, and his understanding family. Although a wealthy gentleman offers to adopt Jiya, he decides to remain poor along with Kino's loving kin. With his new family's help and encouragement, Jiya is able to grieve the loss of his own family, which helps him to face the unknown and years later makes it possible for him to choose to move back to the seaside with his bride, Kino's sister. Powerful.

Burchard, P. *Bimby* (P. Burchard, Illus.). New York: Coward, 1968. Fiction. Ages 8–12. This story is set just before the Civil War. It centers around Bimby, a young slave on St. Simon Island, Georgia, and one-armed Jesse, his old friend, who is a wagon driver. Both are slaves of "Massa" Pierce Butler. One day, as everybody is busy preparing for a big party, Jesse takes Bimby in his dugout canoe and tells him about the rumor that Butler is planning to sell his slaves to the highest bidders and move north. This would mean Bimby would be separated from his mother. Jesse helps the boy realize the hopelessness of being a slave and how important it is to be in charge of oneself. When Jesse gets crushed by his master's wagon, Bimby rows his canoe south—toward freedom or death—pursued by his master's barge. The run for freedom is Bimby's way of paying his last respects to his dead friend Jesse. Although the names of the characters are ficticious, the story is based on historical records, including the auction of the slaves in 1859, and anthropologists are currently conducting archeological investigations of the Butler plantation to further authenticate the record. This story tells vividly about a dark side of United States history and the terrors of being enslaved. At the same time it introduces the reader to a meaning of life and death in a context that is unfamiliar to young North American readers today. A deeply touching story that speaks eloquently about the courage of the human spirit.

Byars, B. *Good-bye, Chicken Little*. New York: Harper, 1979. Fiction. Ages 8–12. Ever since his father was killed in an accident in a coal mine, Jimmie is possessed by a terrible fear. As a kind of self-punishment, he calls himself

"Chicken." Then one day, in Jimmie's presence, his uncle Pete drowns. This tragedy adds a deep sense of guilt to the fear Jimmie has been trying to cope with—a heavy burden for young Jimmie to carry. Fortunately, the offbeat family clan all get together, and their rough and roguish ways cheer Jimmie. His pride to be one of the "Little clan" helps him regain his self-confidence and assuage his guilt. At this time, also, an old friendship that seemed lost is renewed. The story is in many ways very funny, providing a good counterbalance to the stark reality of the two deaths and their impact on the boy. Sensitive and comforting. The author makes a good case for the need for and effectiveness of the family as an emotional support group.

Callen, L. *The deadly mandrake* (L. Johnson, Illus.). Boston: Little, Brown, 1978. Fiction. Ages 9–14. This is a suspenseful story about evil forces presumably emanating from a mandrake, a canelike plant the roots of which spread to resemble arms, legs, and a head. The plant has been used in primitive societies for casting spells. Among a number of unusual happenings in Four Corners, Jeremy Nix, who uproots the plant, gets sick and dies. Aside from the mystery that keeps the reader glued to the book, the story gives a detailed account of early death customs in this country that include the building of the coffin, preparing the body, the procession from the home, the burial, and the participation by the entire community in the funeral rite. This description is interesting and valuable.

Carrick, C. *The accident.* New York: Seabury, 1976. Fiction. Ages 5–8. When a child's beloved pet dies, sorrow is often accompanied by anger and guilt, especially when the pet dies in an accident. That is what happens to Christopher's dog, Bodger. Bodger is killed by a pickup truck near their summer cottage as they are on their way to join Christopher's parents. The little boy has a hard time believing that his father cannot "fix" Bodger and make him well again. Christopher is furious with the truck driver even though the driver is very compassionate. Most of all, Christopher feels guilty and blames himself for the death of his pet. Why had he not taken a different road? Could he have prevented the accident by calling Bodger? His father should not have buried Bodger without him, but Christopher is comforted when they canoe down the creek together and choose a suitable stone for Bodger's grave. Enfolded in his father's arms, Christopher is able to cry. A touching, realistic story with good illustrations.

Cleaver, V., & Cleaver, B. *Where the lilies bloom*. Philadelphia: Lippincott, 1969. Fiction. Age 12 and over. Mary Call Luther, age 14, lives in the mountains of North Carolina with her sharecropper father, two sisters, and a younger brother. Father knows he is dying and pleads with Mary Call to promise she will bury him secretly and keep the family together. When he dies, Mary Call carries through her promise and so prevents the Welfare Department from separating the children. Mary Call's courage and determination get the family through the harsh winter. Fortunately, Mary's older sister, who is 18, decides to get married to Kiser Pease, who helps the family stay together. A fine story. Well written.

Cleaver, V., & Cleaver, B. *Grover*. Philadelphia: Lippincott, 1970. Fiction. Age 9 and over. This sensitive story is about 10-year-old Grover who has to learn to cope in his own groping ways with the changes that the suicide of his ailing mother brings about. Grover's father is too grief-stricken to be of any help to his son. Both Grover and his father, along with the reader, are confronted with the question: Does a person have the duty to endure life no matter how hard the suffering and pain? Grover finds out that there is no simple formula for overcoming grief. It takes much time; one needs friends and maturity, particularly when a suicide is involved. A valuable book for young and older readers.

Cleaver, V., & Cleaver, B. *A little destiny*. New York: Lothrop, 1979. Fiction. Age 12 and over. Set in a small Georgia community at the turn of the century, the story is about 14-year-old Lucy who is determined to find her father's killer and to bring wealth to her poverty-stricken family. Somewhat melodramatic. Lucy, the main character, is not quite believable. The novel is not on a par with the author's other oustanding books, *Grover* and *Where the lilies bloom*, but better than many books on the market for children in their early teens.

Coburn, J. *Anne and the sand dobbies.* New York: Seabury, 1967. Fiction. Ages 8–12. Danny tells of his encounters with death in this gentle and deeply religious book. He tells about his sister Anne, who dies in her sleep of a respiratory infection, and about Bonnie, his dog, who runs away and is found frozen to death. With the help of a neighbor and imaginary characters, the sand dobbies, Danny learns to understand the essence of spiritual life, the presence of God, and that Anne resides in a place of love called heaven. A very comforting book. Most valuable for children raised in the Christian faith.

Coerr, E. *Sadako and the thousand paper cranes* (R. Himler, paintings). New York: Putnam's 1977. Nonfiction. Ages 12–14. Sadako Sasaki died on October 25, 1955, as a result of leukemia caused by the atomic bombing of Hiroshima 10 years earlier. This book tells about the last year of her life, the time following the diagnosis of her illness. In Japan, the crane is a symbol of longevity, and there is an old legend that the gods will give health to a sick person who makes 1,000 paper cranes. Before her death, Sadako folded 644 paper cranes. Afterward her classmates finished the remaining 356. Later they also collected and published her letters (on which this book is based), and eventually a monument was erected to her memory in Hiroshima's Peace Park. This is a gentle and touching story of death in another culture.

Coffin, M. *Death in early America.* New York: Nelson, 1976. Nonfiction. Age 12 and over. This is a reference work that describes artifacts such as tombstones, caskets, and mourning paraphernalia and explains how they are reflections of their culture and times. Interesting.

Cohen, B. *Thank you, Jackie Robinson.* New York: Lothrop, 1974. Fiction. Ages 8–11. This is a well-written story of the slowly developing and deepening friendship between 12-year-old Sam Greene and the elderly black cook, Davy. Both Sam and Davy are interested in sports, and both have the same hero, whose career they follow together: the black baseball player, Jackie Robinson. When Davy dies from a heart attack, Sam mourns the death of his friend. Because his friendship had been strong, the pain of loss is intense for Sam. The reader becomes deeply involved in Sam's pain and grief.

Colman, H. *Sometimes I don't love my mother.* New York: Morrow, 1977. Fiction. Age 12 and over. Following her father's heart attack and sudden death, 17-year-old Dallas finds herself having to cope both with her own grief and with her mother's clinging dependence. To help her mother, Dallas sets aside plans to go away to college but is then caught up in resentment, anger, and the ensuing feelings of guilt. The publisher's note says that in 1957 the author "turned to writing books for teenage girls." This is very much a book for teen-age girls.

Cooney, B. *Cock Robin.* New York: Scribner's, 1965. Fiction. Ages 6–9. This story of a robin, his happy marriage and sudden death caused by an accident, is written in poetic form. It won the 1959 Caldecott Medal. The story is accompanied by beautiful drawings. The death of Cock Robin and his funeral are described realistically and movingly. An appealing book.

Corley, E. A. *Tell me about death. Tell me about funerals.* Santa Clara, Calif.: Grammatical Sciences, 1973. Nonfiction. Ages 8–12. The author, a funeral director and embalmer, explains to a girl whose grandfather has died what happens in funerals. The book deals with the function of a funeral home, the embalming process, caskets, hearses, various types of burials, even the possibility of planning one's own funeral. Such detailed information is what children in this age range often request and seldom get. Amid all this factual information are words of comfort given by the parents. Even some humor is injected, as when the girl is confused about the role of "polar bears" [pallbearers] in a funeral. Valuable.

Cormier, R. *The chocolate war.* New York: Pantheon, 1974. Fiction. Age 12 and over. Jerry Renault's mother has recently died from cancer; his father seems to be sleep-walking through life and shift work as a pharmacist. Then, when Jerry enters a New England Catholic Prep school, he becomes involved with a secret student organization and finds himself under pressure from them and from the school's sadistic assistant headmaster to take part in a fund-raising drive. Can he refuse to sell the candy? "Do I dare disturb the universe?" Jerry's self-assertion has unanticipated and chilling consequences. Like its successors, *I am the cheese* and *After the first death,* this carefully-crafted story explores the dark and complex sides of human behavior.

Cunningham, J. *Burnish me bright.* New York: Pantheon, 1970. Fiction. Ages 10-14. This is a moving story about a mute orphan boy and his short apprenticeship to a dying old man who once was the world's greatest mime. It is set in a small village in the south of France. The story has two main themes. One is that adjusting to being different and handicapped is difficult and requires great strength and courage. The second theme is death. Both are handled with unembellished directness and poignancy. Beautifully written.

Cunningham, J. *Wings of the morning* (K. Peake, Photographer). Los Angeles: Golden Gate Junior Books, 1971. Fiction. Ages 8-12. The photographer's young daughter encounters a "sleeping" bird that is actually dead. This is the girl's first experience with death. The explanations and comfort offered are subtle and symbolic. The young reader is not clearly confronted with death as distinct from sleep. With adult help, however, this clarification can be achieved. Otherwise this book is beautiful with exceptionally good photographs and poetic language. A sensitive story.

Cunningham, J. *Tuppenny.* New York: Dutton, 1978. Fiction. Ages 12-14. A mysterious young girl named Tuppenny comes to a small town where there is much guilt and hatred. The minister's daughter is dead, supposedly a suicide; the older daughter of the factory owner has run away; and the couple who own the café have put their retarded child in an institution. After helping the latter two families to achieve some self-understanding and reconciliation, Tuppenny exposes the evil in the minister. A disconcerting story from the well-known author of *Dear rat* and *Drop dead,* etc.

De Bruyn, M. G. *The beaver who wouldn't die.* Chicago: Follett, 1975. Fiction. Ages 6-9. Cyrus, a beaver who lives in the north woods, is granted through magic his wish never to die.

As he keeps on growing and becomes larger and larger, and particularly as he sees his peers and even his children and grandchildren die, he feels out of place and out of time, gets very lonely and depressed, and wishes he could die. Fortunately, his wish to die is granted, and he happily joins his loved ones in a warm pool, where he hopes to stay forever. A very creative story with colorful and interesting illustrations. The story has an important message about the naturalness of the life cycle. Very well written.

De Paola, T. *Nana Upstairs and Nana Downstairs.* New York: Putnam's, 1973. Fiction. Preschool to 7. This low-key and simply written story depicts with great ease and care the loving relationships four-year-old Tommy has with his great-grandmother (Nana Upstairs) who is 94 years old and bedridden and his grandmother (Nana Downstairs). When Nana Upstairs dies, Tommy is very sad. His mother explains what it means to be dead in a way that is straightforward and honest: "Nana Upstairs won't be here anymore and won't come back except in your memory." Later Tommy's grandmother gets sick and moves upstairs, and then she dies, too. But Tommy's belief that both Nanas are upstairs—in heaven—is comforting when he is confronted with the inevitability of death. The pictures vividly portray feelings and serve well to underscore the story.

Dexter, P. *The emancipation of Joe Tepper.* Nashville: Nelson, 1976. Fiction. Age 12 and over. Joe Tepper has had more than his share of problems for a 15-year-old. He has no father; his mother drinks heavily; and Joe has been on his own for a long time. The family is in financial straits. The money Joe makes on his paper route is just enough to pay for the rent. Then Joe's mother is killed in an accident. Joe is shocked, angry, and distraught. Even though his mother had not been "good" by normal standards, Joe loved her very much, and he misses her and deeply grieves her death. But Joe will not let the social worker take him to a foster home. He will not give up his paper route and his part-time job at the bowling alley. The story tells of Joe's courage, independence, and strong sense of responsibility in the face of hardships and grief. A suspenseful, realistic, and moving story.

Dixon, P. *A time to love—a time to mourn* (Originally published as *May I cross your golden river?*). New York: Scholastic, 1975. Fiction. Age 14 and over. At 18, Jordon Phillips discovers he is slowly dying of the same muscular disorder that killed the famous Yankee baseball player Lou Gehrig. The book vividly describes Jordon's and his family's reaction of shock, anguish, and pain. The reader is not spared details of the pain and the progressive weakness that Jordon experiences, but the reader is also permitted to share Jordon's innermost thoughts and feelings and his interactions with his family and friends. The loving, caring support of his family helps Jordon to prepare himself and them for his death. This is a moving book by a gifted and sensitive writer that depicts masterfully a painful reality but also portrays the power of love to help overcome fears and anxiety and cope with death at an early age.

Dixon, P. *Skipper.* New York: Atheneum, 1979. Fiction. Age 12 and over. A sequel to *May I cross your golden river?* After his brother's death, 14-year-old Skipper sets off from Colorado in search of the father he has never known. The boy never finds this elusive and irresponsible parent, but he does discover four generations of his family in Llangollen, a small North Carolina town. There are tensions in Llangollen, and Skipper's encounters are not all without difficulties (including the death of his great-grandfather); but in the end, he finds a way to go forward with his own life.

Dobrin, A. *Scat!* New York: Four Winds, 1971. Fiction. Ages 6–9. This story deals with a child's emotions and attempts to cope with the loss through death of his beloved grandmother. The boy Scat loves music. He also remembers at the right moment his grandmother's advice: "Listen to what your heart says . . . not your head." He leaves the funeral services, goes to a quiet spot near his grandmother's grave, takes his harmonica out of his pocket and begins to play. This special personal memorial allows him to express his sadness and gives him comfort. A very touching story.

Farley, C. *The garden is doing fine.* New York: Atheneum, 1975. Fiction. Ages 6–8. This book describes the impact of parental death on a young child. Corrie's father is dying of cancer. Corrie and her mother refuse to accept this. Corrie

recalls former happier times and is outraged at the injustice
of her father's suffering. She prays for him and thinks of
him often, but another part of her is also aware of boys,
games, and school activities. Finally, when she can no longer
deny the imminence of her father's death, she is consoled by
the realization that his kindness and love will always be
remembered and will live on through her memory.

Fassler, J. *My grandpa died today* (S. Kranz, Illus.). New York:
Human Sciences, 1971. Fiction. Preschool to 8. This beautifully written story is about a little boy David who, in
narrative form, tells about his beloved grandfather's death
and how he feels about it, how those around him feel, what
they do, and particularly how caring and understanding they
are toward David. David's grandfather had taught him many
things and had shared his thoughts about life and death. One
day he had said: "David, I am getting very old now. And
surely I cannot live forever . . . but I am not afraid to
die . . . because I know that you are not afraid to live." With
this memory, David is better able to cope with his grief and
can get on with life. An essential part of this warm and
comforting story are the exceptional illustrations that vividly
depict in simple strokes the emotions of love, sadness, shock,
the gentleness of comfort, and, yes, the joy of life. A must.

Feagles, A. M. *The year the dreams came back.* New York:
Atheneum, 1973. Fiction. Ages 10–12. Nell hardly knew her
mother. Yet she is guilt-ridden over her mother's suicide and
possessed by fear. When her father decides to remarry,
Nelly's barely repressed feelings come to the surface and
threaten to overwhelm her. Happily, her relationship with a
young man intensifies, and a new girl friend gives support;
surprisingly quickly Nell's depression turns into happiness.
The characters are well developed. The author lightens much
of the gloom and despair by a light touch in style and a
realistic, natural dialogue.

Fisher, L. E. *The death of Evening Star: The diary of a young
New England whaler.* New York: Doubleday, 1972. Fiction.
Ages 10–14. Jeremiah Poole is 14 when his father, a
preacher, dies and leaves his family penniless. Jeremiah is
indentured as a cabin boy to a whaling ship, *Evening Star.*

The book tells of the hardship Jeremiah endures on the high seas, of rough men he encounters, and of the excitement and skill of catching a whale. While in port, Jeremiah runs a high fever and is hustled off the ship to stay with an elderly couple. For a while he is supected of having the plague. The *Evening Star* runs into a storm and goes down with all hands. All this happens in 1841; then, 100 years later, Jeremiah's diary-log wrapped in oilskin mysteriously shows up and is handed to the narrator by an old lighthouse keeper. This is an exciting and engrossing story of high adventure at sea, where death is always close by and accepted stoically. An important focus in this book is the struggle between good and evil forces in men. Most impressive and artistic are the black-and-white drawings by the author, who has illustrated more than 200 children's books.

Fitzhugh, L., & Scoppettone, S. *Bang bang you're dead* (L. Fitzhugh, Illus.). New York: Harper, 1969. Fiction. Preschool to 7. This little book is about James, Timothy, Stanley, and Bert, who dress in their Indian outfits, soldier suits, and cowboy boots to play their games of "Bang Bang You're Dead" almost daily. They fire their make-believe bullets and throw their make-believe rocks and "take a hill" near their homes. The end of the battle for the hill ends with all four little boys lying "dead" on the ground, and then they troop off for a snack. One day there are four frowning strangers on the hill and an argument begins about whose hill it is and who can play there. A war is declared. At 3 p.m. the next day, the war begins. This time the hitting is real, and real blood flows, and everyone gets hurt. That is when the boys decide that having a war is not fun. "Bang, bang, you're dead" happily is not true. The authors portray very effectively how a group of young children discover the seriousness of war and the unreality of make-believe death. The drawings are very well done. They underscore the message and add a richness and vividness that make this little book even more attractive.

Forrai, M. S. *A look at death.* Minneapolis: Lerner, 1978. Nonfiction. Ages 8–10. The photographs are by Forrai, but the text is by Anders. The book is part of the Lerner

Awareness Series (the foreword is by Robert C. Slater, Professor/Director of the Department of Mortuary Science at the University of Minnesota) aimed at making children aware of dying, death, and our death customs. This, the author-photographer is ambitiously trying to accomplish in 16 black-and-white photographs. Some of the photographs are excellent, but others are ambiguous or misleading. The text that accompanies each photograph is very well written; it makes this little book worth reading.

Gardam, J. *The summer after the funeral.* New York: Macmillan, 1973. Fiction. Age 11 and over. The three children are sent off to grieve alone after the death of their father, while the mother does *her* grieving separately. The story poignantly depicts the impact of a parent's death on a teen-ager. Described are all the feelings of anger, denial, frustration, loneliness, and eventually acceptance after an extraordinary summer following the father's death. The various responses to grief are handled perceptively and sensitively. Through all the sadness, the message is hopeful and life affirming.

Glaser, D. *The diary of Trilby Frost.* New York: Holiday House, 1976. Fiction. Age 14 and over. Trilby Frost is 13 when her father gives her a diary in which to write her experiences and feelings. At first, Trilby's entries are sporadic. Trilby only writes when something awful happens, and—unfortunately—Trilby finds much to write. First her father dies, leaving Trilby and her family bereft and in financial need. A boarder is taken in to supplement the meager family income; but that turns into tragedy as he makes Katherine, Trilby's older sister, pregnant, then moves away. Before he does, however, Caleb, Trilby's little brother, is killed trying to ride the boarder's horse. Caleb's death is very difficult for Trilby. She confides to her diary the guilt she feels about the many times she was annoyed with him, about how often she wished him away or dead. She also is angry with God for taking away both her father and brother. Then Katherine miscarried at six months of pregnancy, and this death is quite confusing to Trilby. After all, everybody was unhappy about this unwanted pregnancy, most of all the young mother. Yet now she is grieving. Through all these harrowing experiences, Trilby is able to share her feelings not only with an unresponsive diary but with a flesh-and-blood friend Saul, a half-breed Indian who lives on a neighboring farm. Trilby and Saul are childhood friends and turn to each other for understanding. But even this friend is torn away from her as Saul dies as a result of a wagon accident and is buried on his 17th birthday. There is almost too much to bear for one growing girl in this story, set at the turn of this century. Yet, the story is hopeful in that Trilby is able to cope with her losses and become more mature in the process.

Greenberg, J. *A season in-between.* New York: Farrar, 1979. Fiction. Age 12 and over. Carrie Singer is in between many things. She is a seventh grader growing into young adulthood and her first relationship with a boy friend; she is also one of the few Jewish students at an expensive private school for girls in St. Louis. More important, she is between the diagnosis of her father's cancer in spring and his death that summer; she is further constrained by her own mourning and the needs of her mother, who is now trying to continue to operate the family shoe factory. Carrie is resilient enough to survive these pressures and to begin to see the wisdom of the old rabbinical tale about turning scratches on a jewel into a beautiful design.

Greene, C. C. *Beat the turtle drum.* New York: Viking, 1976. Fiction. Ages 9-13. This beautifully crafted story is about Joss and her older sister Kate. Both love horses, and with enough money saved they rent a horse for one week. Kate, who narrates the story, describes it as the happiest week of their lives until Joss falls from a tree and breaks her neck. Joss's death stuns and paralyzes the family. Mother lies in bed sedated with tranquilizers; Father stays drunk; and 13-year-old Kate is left alone in her pain and grief until her older cousin Mona, the wife of the man who rented the horses, provides comfort. The story ends at the height of grief, but Kate's ability to express her feelings in poetry suggests that she will be able to cope. A realistic and sensitive story.

Grimes, N. *Growin'* (C. Lilly, Illus.). New York: Dial, 1977. Fiction. Ages 12-14. Pump—short for Pumpkin, Yolanda

Jackson's nickname—is a young black girl whose world seems to collapse when her father dies in an automobile accident. He had always been the one who had seemed to understand her and her poetry. After his death, Pump's mother moves them to a new neighborhood, where Pump strikes up an unlikely friendship with Jim Jim, the class bully. Their adventures help Pump through a hard, lonely time until she accidentally discovers that her mother had also tried to write poetry as a young girl. Lack of success condemned Pump's mother to a career as a typist, but the shared interest brings them together again. Unusual for the author's insights into the life and feelings of a black girl and for the eight drawings that highlight key events in the text.

Grollman, E. A. *Talking about death: A dialogue between parent and child.* (G. Héau, Illus.). Boston: Beacon, 1976. Non-fiction. Preschool to 6. This is a new edition of the author's 1970 book by the same title. In this new edition the "Parents' Guide" is expanded to include various ways of using the book, of helping parents themselves come to acknowledge death and grief. This book is for children to read or to have read to them. The author discusses death in an honest, simple, straightforward manner. He insists that the reader understands that dead is *dead.* There is no flinching from the facts, no silence in response to the child's questions. At the same time, the book is warm, loving, sensitive, and tender. Gisela Héau's incredibly beautiful illustrations underscore the text and create a hopeful mood. This is one of the best nonfiction books about death for young children on the market. A must for parents with small children.

Grollman, E. A. *Living when a loved one has died.* Boston: Beacon, 1977. Nonfiction. Age 14 and over. Although the intent of the well-known author and rabbi was to write this book for bereaved adults, it is equally suited for mature adolescents and youths. The book skillfully blends new scientific information about the grieving process with the compassion and gentleness of a friend, counselor, or pastor, making this book particularly helpful to those who have just experienced the death of a loved one. The language is simple and direct, in keeping with the author's other book, *Talking about death.* Some unusually good black-and-white photographs add to the impact of the book.

Gunther, J. *Death be not proud: A memoir.* New York: Harper, 1949. Nonfiction. Age 14 and over. This first-person narrative gives a moving account of the author's son's 15-month fight with a brain tumor. Johnny is 15 years old when the diagnosis is made. His determination and courage are inspiring. His dream is to go to Harvard University, and his brilliance and willpower help him to keep up with his studies. His need for hope and for living each day fully are vividly shown. He continues to do laboratory experiments while confined to bed and studies diligently to prepare for the college board examinations even at the time when his tumor is progressing relentlessly. The reader is confronted with the difficulty the parents have in acknowledging that their son is dying and their efforts to keep the truth from him. But it is Johnny who protects his parents. Interspersed in the narrative are letters and notes written by Johnny that are deeply touching and make the reader want to laugh and cry. Johnny's strength of spirit is an inspiration.

Hamilton-Paterson, J., & Andrews, C. *Mummies: Death and life in ancient Egypt.* New York: Penguin, 1979. Nonfiction. Age 12 and over. Embalming or mummification practices in ancient Egypt occurred over a period lasting some 2,700 years. Although the most prominent forms of these practices applied mainly to a small minority of the population—members of the royal or upper class and later some middle-class people, but never to the large body of ordinary people—they still excite widespread interest and curiosity today. Despite some confusing theology and technical detail, together with an obviously British tone and vocabulary, that interest will be well satisfied in this thorough and informative study. Fascinating reading for adults and adolescents alike!

Harnden, R. P. *The high pasture.* Boston: Houghton Mifflin, 1964. Fiction. Age 12 and over. Thirteen-year-old Tim is sent away from home to spend the summer with his great-aunt Kate on her ranch because his mother is ill in the hospital. When Aunt Kate's old dog dies early in the summer, Tim becomes apprehensive and anxious. Tim's anxiety must be blamed on his family's failure to inform him of the nature and seriousness of his mother's illness. In talking to his father, Tim learns that his mother is going to die but that the parents wanted to protect him because they love him. This story describes well what parents ought *not* to do in such a situation. Fortunately, there is much mutual sharing of grief, and Tim is surprisingly tolerant, given the circumstances. Written for children but profitable reading for adults, particularly parents.

Harris, A. *Why did he die?* Minneapolis: Lerner, 1965. Nonfiction. Preschool to 6. A mother explains death to her young son Scott, whose friend Jim has lost his grandfather. This mother is open and honest in her attempt to answer her child's questions. She likens death to the leaves falling in autumn but with new ones to come in the spring. Another way she explains death is by using as an example a worn-out motor. The whole story is in poetic form and has beautiful illustrations to match. The emphasis is on the concept that, though loved ones die, their memories will not. Warm, frank, and hopeful. A good example of how death can be handled with a child of kindergarten age.

Härtling, I. *Oma* (A. Bell, Trans., from German; J. Ash, Illus.). New York: Harper, 1977. Fiction. Ages 8–12. The orphaned five-year-old Kalle is sent to live with Oma (German for grandma) in Munich. During the following years Kalle and Oma have to deal with a number of people—welfare workers, teachers, other old people. The story is ably crafted to show how child and grandparent learn to adjust to one another and become fond of one another after many episodes of anger, frustration, mistrust, and misunderstanding. The narration is natural, simple, and flows well. The author captures the difference in patterns and styles of communication between the young and the old. The reader receives additional insights about Oma's personality through her first-person comments that are set off at the end of each of the 15 brief chapters of the book. Throughout, an apparent message to the reader is "You're as young as you feel" (perhaps this book should be recommended for adults as well as children). The black-and-white drawings effectively underscore the light and comic events. Excellent.

Hughes, P. R. *Dying is different.* Mahomet, Ill.: Mech Mentor Educational, 1978. Nonfiction. Preschool to 8. This beautiful book by a gifted writer, artist, and psychologist is intended to promote discussion of death between adults and very young children. The 18 children's pages use drawings, strong colors, and poems to present a graduated succession of living and dead states in flowers, ants, fish, a cat, and a grandmother, followed by vivid thematic depictions of the inevitability of death, its justification, remembering, acceptance, grief, funerals, cemeteries, and the importance of love during life. An introduction and concluding remarks for parents and teachers suggest questions and guidelines for discussion. A very helpful resource for adult-child interactions, one that adults can read alone or share with children. Available in both a large instructional edition designed to stand upright by itself and a smaller personal edition in standard book format.

Hunter, J. *A sound of chariots.* New York: Harper, 1972. Fiction. Age 12 and over. Bridie McShane experiences a happy childhood in Scotland that comes to a sudden halt: Her father dies. Bridie had been her father's favorite child, and she had loved her father immensely. She is grief stricken. From her father's death on, her life is marred by the pain and sorrow of her loss. Her thoughts become morbid as she gropes to adjust. Eventually she discovers that she loves poetry, and she begins to write and express her thoughts and feelings and thereby learns to cope. Although this story is lacking in action and adventure (the title is misleading), it conveys convincingly a problem seldom discussed in other stories with a similar theme: the problem of delayed or prolonged grief.

Hunter, M. *The third eye.* New York: Harper, 1979. Fiction. Ages 12–14. According to the Ballinford doom, for hundreds of years no first-born son has lived to inherit the Scottish title Earl of Ballinford. In 1935, a young girl, Janet (Jinty) Morrison, is asked to give testimony in an inquiry into the death of the old earl, which occurred on the day his only son reached the age of 21. Was the death a tragic accident, or did the earl die by his own hand to break the curse? Told as a flashback over a three-year period, this well-executed novel introduces the Morrison family: a quiet father, a strong-willed mother who is determined that her girls will get what she herself has missed in life, two rebellious older sisters, and Jinty. Jinty gains the earl's friendship by her honesty and intuitive sense of inward feelings (her "third eye"), traits that also appear in her artwork in school and in the way she helps a blind boy to "see" through tactile analogues before his death. A story of adventure and foreboding in which Jinty's wisdom helps her troubled family and village.

Huntsberry, W. E. *The big hang-up.* New York: Lothrop, 1970. Fiction. Age 12 and over. High school seniors Corey, Rick, and Jim are triple-dating for an important fall dance. The night of the dance, Rick drives his mother's new Lincoln. Later in the evening they drink beer, and Corey, feeling high, urges Rick to see how fast the new car can go. They have an accident and one of the girls dies. Blaming himself for the accident, Corey is sick with grief and guilt. When he returns to school he learns that Rick is blamed for the accident and drops out of school. Corey slowly comes to the painful realization that he must bear his guilt, for people are responsible for their own behavior. A starkly realistic story. The reader is left with the suggestion that Corey finally is able to cope with the tragic event, recognizing that no amount of guilt and self-blame is going to bring back the girl. A hard lesson learned, and Corey will become a responsible adult.

Hyde, M. O., & Forsyth, E. H. *Suicide: The hidden epidemic.* New York: Watts, 1978. Nonfiction. Age 12 and over. A significant recent increase in the incidence of suicide among young people makes this an important subject for them to study and understand. This book, written by an experienced children's writer and a child psychiatrist who have collaborated on two previous books, offers factual and theoretical information as well as practical advice. The writing style is clear, and the presentation is aided by numerous subheadings within each chapter. The book concludes with a list of crisis intervention centers in the United States and two pages of suggestions for further reading. An authoritative study for young people that can also be read with profit by adults.

Jones, M. A. *Tell me about heaven* (M. Cooper, Illus.). Chicago: Rand McNally, 1956. Nonfiction. Ages 6–8. This book is exceptionally good in helping children understand death and what happens afterward. It is based on the Christian belief system. The author's insight into children's thoughts and concerns is impressive. Many parents of small children are probably confronted with similar questions: Is heaven above the sky? Will dogs go to heaven? What is heaven like? Can we come back from heaven? What do people do in heaven? The answers provided to the questions are appropriate for chidren with a Christian background without being contrary to scientific fact. The writing is beautifully simple and appealing. This book would be helpful to parents who have difficulty dealing with such questions.

Kantrowitz, M. *When Violet died.* New York: Parents' Magazine Press, 1973. Fiction. Preschool to 8. When Amy's and Eva's pet bird Violet dies, the children plan a funeral and a memorial. They invite other children to participate in the ceremony, which includes singing, recital of poetry, and serving punch. The children behave very much as adults do when a death occurs, but their grief is quickly resolved when they discover that Blanche, their cat, is pregnant. The children excitedly await the birth of the kittens. Kantrowitz very skillfully shows the comfort that is derived from the knowledge that life is a continuous process. The story also shows that funerals do not *have* to be all sad. Written with warmth, compassion, and insight into children's thoughts and feelings.

Kaplan, B. *The empty chair.* New York: Harper, 1978. Fiction. Ages 6–9. This is a story of Jewish family life, with Becky Levine as the central character. Although Becky's life with her brother Saul and Mama and Papa is basically good, she secretly yearns for the luxuries her friends can afford and she cannot. One day Mama announces that she is pregnant, and the family is sparked by the joy of anticipation. Unfortunately, both Mama and the baby die during childbirth. The story skillfully and touchingly depicts the emptiness in the hearts of the surviving family members and the well-intentioned actions of relatives and friends. Eventually Papa remarries, and Becky has to learn to accept the new mother.

Kerr, J. *A small person far away.* New York: Coward, 1979. Fiction. Age 12 and over. Judith Kerr's three autobiographic novels follow Anna and her family after they leave Germany just before Hitler's election in 1933. They flee because they are ethnic Jews and Papa is a prominent anti-Nazi writer and intellectual. *When Hitler stole Pink Rabbit* (1972) covers a two-year period during which 9-year-old Anna, her 12-year-old brother, and their parents move from Berlin, first to Switzerland and then to Paris. *The other way round* (1975) follows teen-age Anna as she develops her artistic abilities in London during the war. Throughout both of these books, Anna's young perspective is fresh and unique; loss and deprivation lead her to hard work and well-earned growth. In *A small person far away,* Anna, who is now in her early thirties, newly married to a successful television writer, and beginning her own writing career in London, is called back to Berlin in the middle of the Hungarian and Suez crises in 1956, where her now-widowed mother has attempted suicide. During the six days of her visit, a welter of thoughts and feelings tumble about in Anna's mind—dominated always by the warmth of her memories of gentle Papa and the intensity of her image of Mama. Eventually, Mama recovers and seems to be on the way to resuming life with her friend Konrad, and Anna returns to England to discover that she is pregnant. Judith Kerr has a marvelous ability for deft characterization and evocative description. All three of these books are splendid reading for younger and older readers alike; perhaps the last deals most intimately with themes of life and death.

Kidd, R. *That's what friends are for.* Nashville: Nelson, 1978. Fiction. Ages 12–14. Two boys meet and become close friends in seventh grade in a California junior high school. A year later one of them falls ill. Scott is not told the truth about his condition, but Gary accidentally learns that his friend is dying of leukemia. Gary is bewildered by these events and by the atmosphere of secretiveness. He is especially shaken by his own inability to help his friend—he even stays away from the hospital during the last two weeks before Scott's death—or to find solace at the funeral. Gary shares his story and feelings in this book: "I have to tell someone."

Klagsbrun, F. *Too young to die: Youth and suicide.* Boston: Houghton Mifflin, 1976; New York: Pocket Books, 1977. Nonfiction. Age 14 and over. This is the first book about suicide among adolescents and college students that was written to be read by young people as well as by their parents, counselors, and teachers. Its three parts deal, respectively, with the realities of suicide among the young—statistics, common myths, suicide as communication, the role of depression or psychosis, and uncounted or "chronic" suicides; practical guidelines—"What can you do?—for dealing both with crisis situations and with survivors; and social aspects—sociologic or psychological causes, cultural attitudes, and prevention techniques. Appendixes document the rise in suicide rates among the 15- to 24-year-old age group over the 20-year period from 1954 to 1974 and list many suicide prevention or crisis intervention agencies in the United States. There is also an eight-page bibliography. An excellent resource on a subject that deserves more attention. Valuable for adult reading.

Klein, N. *Sunshine.* New York: Avon, 1974. Nonfiction. Age 16 and over. Kate Hayden is the 19-year-old mother of Jill, who is six months old. Kate has a rare form of bone cancer. After having divorced Jill's father, she finds Sam. They love each other deeply, and they get married. As the cancer progresses, Kate decides to refrain from taking medication, thus shortening her life. Sam does not understand. He accuses her of committing suicide. Kate states her case: Off the drugs she will die more quickly, but she will be capable of feeling and loving. She has much love to give to Sam and Jill. Kate's doctor supports her decision and gives her the tape recorder whose tapes form the basis for the book (and the film). This is a story of love, loneliness, and a need to die with dignity. It is tender and gripping but also painful and starkly realistic.

Klein, S. *The final mystery.* New York: Doubleday, 1974. Nonfiction. Ages 8–13. The author explores the meanings of death for people living in different times and regions and having different religions. The discussion is unique in its emphasis on ways in which people have attempted to fight death through the generations. Studies of people's feelings about death, especially fear, are described as well as burial and funeral customs. Through all of this, the author is able to show that death, like some other events, remains a mystery.

Kübler-Ross, E. *On death and dying.* New York: Macmillan, 1969. Nonfiction. Age 16 and over. Although written for adults, mature adolescents will find this now-classic work informative and humane in its plea to health care givers and family for better understanding, empathy, openness, and care for dying people. The book is largely based on personal interviews the famous physician-psychiatrist conducted with over 400 dying patients at Chicago's Billings Hospital. The book has been translated in many different languages and read by millions. The language is simple and powerful.

Landau, E. *Death: Everyone's heritage.* New York: Messner, 1976. Nonfiction. Age 14 and over. The author, a children's librarian, uses a variety of anecdotes to illustrate issues concerning medical death: euthanasia, terminal care, suicide, cryonics, funerals, cemeteries, and the grief of survivors. With the help of new stories, cross-cultural data, and interviews, the author carefully presents both sides of each issue. This book is informative and thought provoking. The author shows sympathetic insight into the dynamics of suicidal people and the pain of despair.

Langone, J. *Death is a noun: A view of the end of life.* Boston: Little, Brown, 1972; New York: Dell, 1975. Nonfiction. Age 12 and over. This simply and clearly written book presents a broad survey of important aspects and issues concerning death. Using research reports, historical analyses, and human interest stories, the author deals with basic attitudes toward death, euthanasia, abortion, capital punishment, murder, suicide, problems of determining medical death, grief, and the quest for immortality. In addition, various philosophical and religious beliefs about life after death are discussed, such as animism, theism, deism, atheism, Christianity, Judaism, Hinduism, Buddhism, and Islam. Highly instructive. Should have wide appeal not only for young readers but for adults as well. A good companion to Langone's book *Vital signs: The way we die in America.*

Langone, J. *Vital signs: The way we die in America.* Boston: Little, Brown, 1974. Nonfiction. Age 16 and over. In this documentary the author skillfully weaves together a variety of materials: classical quotations, scientific data, legal case material, news reports, and interviews with doctors, nurses, clergy, and dying people and their families. In doing this he reaveals startling facts about the way people die today. The reader is immediately involved in the current dilemma about the definition of death, in the depersonalization of contemporary dying, and in the universal desire for dignity. This book is instructive and humanistic in its plea for greater empathy for the needs of the dying. Indignant and compassionate. A valuable book for mature young readers as well as adults.

Lee, M. S. *Fog.* New York: Seabury, 1972. Fiction. Age 12 and over. This book deals with the grief and sense of loss that Luke experiences at the death of his father, as well as another kind of grief, hurt, and anger he feels when he and his girl friend decide to stop seeing each other. The reader is also drawn into the boy's struggle over his choice of a career and his feelings of guilt about the clubhouse fire. The language is contemporary and attractive. The characters portrayed are vivid and believable.

Lee, R. *The magic moth.* New York: Seabury, 1972. Fiction. Ages 8–11. Ten-year-old Maryanne is the middle child in a family of five, and she has a heart defect. Everything possible has been done, including heart surgery, but now the family is told that Maryanne cannot be cured. The story tells of the love, courage, strength, and support of the Foss family and the problems that had to be overcome in helping each other cope with Maryanne's impending untimely death. A moth bursts from its cocoon as Maryanne dies, and seeds sprout just after her funeral, symbolizing that "life never ends—it just changes," a belief that offers much comfort to both young and old readers. This is a touching story told in a straightforward and unsentimental manner.

L'Engle, M. *Meet the Austins.* New York: Vanguard, 1960. Fiction. Ages 9–12. Vicki Austin is 12 years old, a happy member of a happy family including her older brother John, younger sister Suzy, and little brother Rob. Mother is preparing a gala dinner for Uncle Douglas, who has arrived for a visit. The phone rings, but that is a frequent event at the Austin's as Father is a doctor. But this call is different. It brings the bad news that Uncle Hal has been killed in a plane crash. He was the pilot. Also killed was his copilot, which left his 8-year-old daughter Maggie an orphan. The Austin's take Maggie into their home until her eccentric grandfather can decide what to do with her. The story describes with great sensitivity how Vicki tries to cope with the loss of her favorite uncle and with the deep resentment she feels toward Maggie, who appears to be a spoiled and selfish child but who actually has never had the security and warmth of a family. Eventually, Maggie is accepted to the degree that the Austins hope Maggie's grandfather will let her stay with them, which he finally decides to do. All through the story, one is impressed with the love, insight, and patience of Vicki's parents and with their effectiveness in helping the children to be tolerant of each other and to care. A very readable book by a well-known writer.

L'Engle, M. *A ring of endless light.* New York: Farrar, 1980. Fiction. Age 12 and over. During the summer when she is almost 16, Vicky Austin finds herself with three young men on her hands: Leo, who lives on the island where they are visiting, seeks comfort from her after his father's unexpected death; Zachary, a rich friend whose suicide attempt had inadvertently caused Leo's father's death, tries to make her responsible for his well-being; and Adam, a student of marine biology, discovers that she has telepathic powers that can aid in his experiments with wild dolphins. All the while,

Vicky's minister grandfather is dying of leukemia. As his condition deteriorates, Vicky struggles to overcome her confusion and grief through reading and her own poetry. The book's title (short for "a great ring of pure and endless light") and another line from Henry Vaughan's poetry—"a deep but dazzling darkness"—offer metaphors for eternity that portray the spiritual and moral dimensions underlying life processes. Characters, events, and meanings are skillfully evoked through sensitive writing and careful detail by a prolific and respected writer for children as well as adults.

LeShan, E. *Learning to say good-by: When a parent dies.* New York: Macmillan, 1978. Nonfiction. Age 10 and over. This family counselor and writer speaks to children in a simple, straightforward manner about the problems they face when losing a parent and how these problems may be overcome. The main thrust throughout this helpful and comforting book is the acceptance of the griever as a person who is suffering much pain and disorientation but who is healthy and will be capable of coping by expressing and sharing her or his feelings in open communication with interested and caring adults. The book is well-written, and examples are used to amply illustrate a situation or clarify a point. An informative, nonthreatening, supportive book.

Levit, R. E. *A short life long remembered.* New York: Bantam, 1974. Nonfiction. Age 12 and over. In the midst of her parents' struggles with their own separation, 15-year-old Ellen is diagnosed as having bone cancer. The book is the mother's personal account of her daughter's last two years of life, interspersed with letters and poetry written by Ellen during her illness. Not a literary piece but a believable portrayal.

Lifton, R. and Olson, E. *Living and dying.* New York: Praeger, 1974. Nonfiction. Age 15 and over. The authors discuss the ways in which North Americans have written death out of their culture and sought "immortality" through various symbolic modes of escape. They also note the attitudinal transformation growing out of nuclear fears and national self-confrontation brought on by Vietnam, the assassinations of the 1960s, and other traumatic events. The authors espouse the philosophy that it is better to confront death, risk loss, and live well than to evade life's challenges, sorrows, and joys. They consider experiential transcendence as a means of coping with time and death. A profound and provocative book. Intellectually demanding. Although not specifically written for youths, mature young readers will be challenged and stimulated.

Little, J. *Home from far.* Boston: Little, Brown, 1965. Fiction. Ages 9-12. Jenny's twin brother, Michael, is killed; and soon after the accident Jenny's parents bring two foster children into the home. One of them, named Mike, is Jenny's age. Jenny is deeply hurt and bitterly resents her parents for having brought these other children into their home. She believes her parents have forgotten Michael, and so she withdraws. The period that follows is a difficult one for the family and also for the foster children Hilda and Mike, whose own mother has died. The author sensitively portrays the feelings of grief, loss, anger, and fear of abandonment and shows how sharing one's feelings make them more bearable. Especially valuable for children who have difficulty expressing grief.

Lowry, L. *A summer to die.* Boston: Houghton Mifflin, 1977. Fiction. Ages 10-15. The themes of birth and death are juxtaposed in this story of 13-year-old Meg, her pretty 15-year-old sister Molly, and their parents, who move to the country so that their father can write a book. Lonely at first and jealous of her popular, lively sister, Meg meets and befriends an elderly neighbor and a young couple living nearby. She also begins to recognize and develop her own talents. The sense of tranquility, however, is shattered when Molly becomes terminally ill. As Molly weakens, Meg's overwhelming interest becomes the baby expected by the young neighbors. It is through the drama of their baby's birth at home, with Meg sharing in the experience, that the poignant link between birth and death is made.

Lowry, L. *Autumn Street.* Boston: Houghton Mifflin, 1980. Fiction. Ages 10-14. This, the most recent book by the author of *A summer to die,* demonstrates perhaps even better the author's ability to enter and move freely in the child's worlds of thoughts, dreams, worries, anxieties, and fears. Elizabeth is six years old. Her father has gone off to fight in World War II; and Elizabeth, her mother, sisters, and baby brother go to live with her grandparents on Autumn Street in a small Pennsylvania town. The street ends in a wood that is declared forbidden territory by the adults; it both terrifies and attracts Elizabeth and her friend Charles. One day, humiliated by a gang of boys in the park, Charles wants to demonstrate his courage to Elizabeth and runs toward the woods. Elizabeth tries unsuccessfully to persuade him to stay away, returns home with a fever and a sore throat, and is put to bed. When Charles does not return by nightfall, everyone begins to worry, and he is reported missing. Then the shocking news arrives: Charles has been murdered. Violent death is a reality, and the author has the courage to deal with it and does it sensitively. The story shows in a cryptic yet moving way the extent and quality of comfort given to children by caring adults, even if their worlds may be far apart.

Lundgren, M. *Matt's grandfather* (A. Pyk, Trans.; F. Hald, Illus.). New York: Putnam's, 1972. Fiction. Ages 6–8. Matt and his parents are on the way to visit the little boy's grandfather on his 85th birthday. Grandfather lives in a nursing home; and Matt's parents try to explain that grandfather is senile ("he is almost like a baby again"), that he forgets things and needs nurses to take care of him and the other old people, who may walk in the park but are not allowed out because they might get lost. When Matt arrives, he has his first surprise: the nursing home is like a huge castle with spires and towers, and ivy, and the park is beautiful. When he gets to Room 115, Matt has his second surprise. Grandfather does not look so old at all, and he certainly does not act like a baby. The third surprise remains a secret between Matt and Grandfather. It is an ingenious way Grandfather had discovered to get out of the park and go down to the boats for a while each day and to be back before anybody misses him. This story is simply written, but it speaks eloquently of the problems facing some old people, and it portrays with great tenderness the mutual closeness and warmth possible between the very young and the very old. The colored illustrations are vivid and add greatly to the mood of the story.

Lutters, V. A. *The haunting of Julie Unger.* New York: Atheneum, 1977. Fiction. Age 12 and over. Thirteen-year-old Julie Unger is "haunted" by Papa, her father who has died recently of a heart attack. Julie and Papa had been very close. He had been a photographer, and photography is Julie's hobby. The "haunting" Julie experiences is benign. She copes with her loss by revisiting the places where she and her father had spent time together, such as the river bank on which they had sat, talking and taking pictures of Canada geese. Julie secretly takes up photography again and is angry at her family for "spying" on her in the darkroom. In fact, she does not get along with her family at all, especially not with her grandparents. Julie Unger copes well with her father's death, but she needs to do her grieving alone. After a time, her family begins to understand this, and harmony is reestablished.

Madison, A. *Suicide and young people.* New York: Seabury/ Clarion, 1978. Nonfiction. Age 14 and over. This book discusses possible causes for the rising rate of suicide among young people. The approach is journalistic, with frequent stylized case examples and occasionally confusion over interwoven questions of euthanasia. The concluding list of suicide prevention centers is not comprehensive. On the whole, however, a readable book.

Madison, W. *A portrait of myself.* New York: Random House, 1979. Fiction. Age 14 and over. Pressure from a broken home and a favorite teacher's rejection can drive a high school student to suicide. Catherine d'Amato is a sensitive, artistic 16-year-old whose father left their Connecticut home four years earlier and whose mother wants her to be popular and to take practical courses. Her large Italian family sometimes seems to stifle her individuality. Catherine is an artist who wants to be someone other than herself and who mistakenly thinks a cool, Nordic gym teacher would be a good role model for her. When the imitation fails and the pressures become too great, Catherine attempts suicide but does not succeed. This leads to a visit with her immigrant grandparents, who remind her of her own good qualities and who give her an example of the courage to be oneself. This is good writing for young people, a well-delineated sketch of character without clichés or false emotions.

Mann, P. *There are two kinds of terrible.* New York: Doubleday, 1977. Fiction. Ages 9-12. The first kind of terrible, breaking one's arm just as summer vacation starts, is shown to be far easier for a grade school child than the illness and death of a parent. During his mother's hospitalization, Robbie Farley gets little information or support from his uncommunicative father. An only child, Rob has always been very close to his mother. Now, father and son each withdraw into isolation, which only intensifies anxieties and anguish and makes them almost unbearable to each other. Only after his mother's death can Robbie and his father reach out to each other and share their loss and warm memories of the woman they both loved. A very effective portrait from the child's viewpoint, by the author of many other books including the well-known story of divorce, *My dad lives in a downtown hotel.*

Mazer, N. *A figure of speech.* New York: Delacorte, 1973. Fiction. Age 8 and over. This poignant story is about Jenny, a young girl, and her grandfather whom she loves deeply. When she overhears her parents discussing plans to send him to a nursing home, Jenny reports the discussion to her grandfather, and both run away. This results in grandfather's death, which cause the estrangement of Jenny from her parents. Recommended only with parental guidance and discussion of the book, particularly its ending, to reassure the young reader of his or her parents' unconditional love.

Mendoza, G. *The hunter I might have been.* Stamford, Conn.: Astor-Honor, 1968. Fiction. Ages 9-12. An allegory in which startingly brief text and expressionistic photographs cause the reader to recognize and experience the anguish of killing and death and the meaning of love and life.

Miles, B. *The touble with thirteen.* New York: Knopf, 1979. Fiction. Ages 9-13. This story is about two girls turning 13, the difficulties they encounter, and the adjustments they have to make. Mostly, it is about losses and how to cope with them. Rachel's parents are getting a divorce, and Rachel's mother will be moving to New York City to find work. Rachel is going to live with her mother, which means leaving her girl friend Annie. Just as Annie is trying hard to prepare herself for Rachel's leaving, she discovers Nora, her dog, lying helpless under a lilac bush. The dog had begun to cough a few days earlier, and Father did not think it was necessary to take Nora to the verterinarian. But now Nora is wheezing, her body is jerking and twitching in Annie's arms; and no amount of comforting helps. As Nora thumps her tail, trying to please, and looks sadly into Annie's eyes, she gives a quick little gasp and dies. The author relates sensitively how Nora is buried and memorialized and how Annie copes with her anger at Father, her grief and sorrow, and how she is comforted by her parents, brother, and friends. We all experience losses as we grow and change, but good memories can be cherished. An engrossing, well-written story.

Miles, M. *Annie and the old one.* Boston: Little, Brown, 1971. Fiction. Ages 8–12. This is the moving story of Annie, a nine-year-old Navajo girl, and her grandmother who is making preparations for her death. When Annie's grandmother explains that when the new rug is woven and taken from the loom she will be ready to "go to Mother Earth," Annie tries desperately to stop the rug from getting finished. She is told by her grandmother in a gentle way that the "earth from which good things come is where all creatures finally go." This helps Annie see how the entire family, including herself, are part of this life cycle and that death is a part of life. Carefully detailed, beautifully written.

Molloy, A. S. *The girl from two miles high.* New York: Hastings House, 1967. Fiction. Age 12 and over. After her mother's death, 13-year-old Phoebe lives with her father, a mining engineer in the Peruvian mountains. Phoebe loves her father deeply and needs his love particularly since her mother's death. Then one day her father is killed in an avalanche. Phoebe feels that she is left all alone. She is put on a plane to go live with her grandmother. The story tells rather sensitively how Phoebe learns to cope with the loss of her parents and how both she and her grandmother learn to adjust to one another and eventually come to love each other. The reader will find it easy to identify with Phoebe's loss, grief, loneliness, and eventual reestablishment in a new environment. Love is a basic need all people have, young or old. And love helps heal wounds. Good reading.

Moody, R. *Life after life*. St. Simons Island, Ga.: Mockingbird, 1975. Nonfiction. Age 16 and over. In this fascinating book the author reports the results of his interviews with 150 people with near-death experiences. Most had been resuscitated following cardiac arrests. The accounts of out-of-the-body experiences and experiences of meeting dead relatives and a "being of light," all accompanied with an experience of indescribable peace and beauty, are truly amazing. Scientists are still trying to explain these experiences physiologically and psychologically. A courageous book.

Morgan, E. *A manual of death ecucation and simple burial*. Burnsville, N.C.: Celo, 1980. Nonfiction. Age 14 and over. This is the ninth edition of a concise, plainly written pamphlet that provides information about death education; about relating to dying people; and most particularly about memorial societies and their functions; simple burial or cremation; and body, organ, and tissue donation. The author is one of the founders of the Continental Association of Funeral and Memorial Societies. Although not written specifically for youthful readers, this book answers many practical questions that adolescents often ask, and it is written in clear and simple language, making it a valuable resource for them.

Naylor, P. R. *To walk the sky path*. Chicago: Follett, 1973. Fiction. Ages 10-13. Ten-year-old Billie, a Seminole Indian, knows he is a link between two very different worlds. Yet he feels torn between living the traditional way of his grandparents and enjoying the modern conveniences of the white people. He learns all of the Indian stories and legends that he can, but he also feels that going to school is important. When his grandfather dies and is buried in the traditional Indian manner, the boy realizes that an important part of his life is gone. He cherishes the memory of his grandfather and his heritage.

Ness, E. *Sam Bangs and moonshine.* New York: Holt, 1966. Fiction. Preschool to age 9. Samantha, called Sam, is a fisherman's daughter who envelops herself in a world of fantasy in which her dead mother becomes a mermaid living in a cave; in which Bang, her cat, can talk and have conversations with her; and in which she has a baby kangaroo as a pet. Her father helps Sam to confront reality and distinguish it from moonshine (her fantasy world). A beautiful, imaginative story, winner of the 1967 Caldecott Medal.

Norris, G. B. *The friendship hedge* (D. Payson, Illus.). New York: Dutton, 1973. Ages 6–9. When Claire receives a guinea pig for her birthday, she is so enthralled that she neglects the nine girls at her party and even forgets the cake. No one is allowed even to touch the guinea pig. Claire's best friend, Alice, is angrier than the others, and she seeks revenge. The story tells of the jealousy Alice feels, how her revenge accidentally leads to the death of the guinea pig, how Claire copes with the loss of her new pet and Alice with her feelings of guilt and remorse. The two girls bury the guinea pig by the Friendship Hedge, and their friendship survives. A well-told story. The illustrations are appealing.

Orgel, D. *Mulberry music.* New York: Harper, 1971. Fiction. Ages 8–12. The efforts of Libby's parents to protect her from the harsh reality of her beloved grandmother's impending death result in turmoil both within the girl and around her. Jenny, searching for Grandma Liza, breaks into her grandmother's home. Sitting down at the piano, she plays the favorite pieces she and Grandma Liza had shared and finds comfort in doing so. After her grandmother's death, a home memorial service is held during which her grandmother's favorite music is played. This is a realistic story that depicts the parents' good intentions as well as their willingness and courage to admit that they made a mistake in the way they handled a crisis. Well written and well worth reading. Also recommended for parents.

Patterson, K. *Bridge to Terabithia.* New York: Crowell, 1977. Fiction. Ages 9–11. Ten-year-old Jess Aarons is a loner, far too talented and sensitive to fit easily into a traditional, isolated, rural Virginia lifestyle. The Burke family moves into the community to escape the rigors of city life, and Jess and Leslie become close friends. Leslie appreciates Jess's art and teaches him that imagination, caring, and love for learning are nothing to be ashamed of. Together they create Terabithia, a private, secret kingdom in the woods where their imaginations rule. The joy turns to tragedy as Leslie is killed in an accident on her way through the woods. Jess's subsequent dealing with her death is realistically and sensitively described.

Peck, R. N. *A day no pigs would die.* New York: Knopf, 1972. Fiction. Age 12 and over. Robert Peck, a 13-year-old Vermont farm boy, has been given a small pig, which he raises as a pet. Haven Peck, Robert's father, is ill and knows he has not long to live. When fall comes and the pig has not had her first heat, Robert recognizes that the family cannot afford to keep the pig. Mr. Peck, a hog butcher by trade, and Robert kill the pig. When Robert understands the difficulty his father had killing the pet, he realizes how much he loves and admires his father. Shortly afterward, Mr. Peck dies. Robert must arrange his father's funeral, and he must learn to cope with the sadness and pain he experiences at his father's death.

Pevsner, S. *And you give ma pain, Elaine.* New York: Seabury/ Clarion, 1978. Fiction. Age 12 and over. Andrea is 13; she has a 16-year-old sister Elaine and a brother Joe, who is a college sophomore. Andrea loves Joe in a special way, but Elaine is a troublemaker who perplexes her parents and keeps the house in turmoil. Andrea resents Elaine's behavior and the way she seems to monopolize their parents' attention. The book follows the many events in Andrea's life. Toward the end, when Elaine seems to be settling down and reestablishing good relationships with her family, Joe is suddenly killed in a motorcycle accident. The family's grief, the funeral, and later events are briefly sketched. Life is rebuilt and goes forward.

Pringle, L. *Death is natural.* New York: Four Winds, 1977. Nonfiction. Ages 8–12. Using as a theme the death of a rabbit hit by a car, the text explains how the rabbit's body is recycled through scavengers and decay. Death is shown as necessary so that elements and atoms can be passed on to other forms of life. Characteristics, genes, extinct species, and the balance of nature are discussed. This book emphasizes death as a natural part of the life cycle—as it affects the world as a whole rather than the individual—and it points at the interdependence of various forms of life. The book does not merely inform by giving the reader a hint of the larger picture; it does much more. It inspires awe.

Rabe, B. *The girl who had no name.* New York: Dutton, 1977. Fiction. Ages 9–12. It is 1936 in southeast Missouri, and Girlie Webster is 12. Following her mother's death, Girlie is sent by Papa to live with one after another of her nine older sisters. Girlie's story traces her efforts to discover why she cannot live with Papa and why he refused to give her a proper name when she was born. There is comedy and mystery in this tale of a young girl's determination and maturation.

Rabin, G. *Changes.* New York: Harper, 1973. Fiction. Age 12 and over. In this keenly perceptive and realistic first-person narrative, Chris, who still grieves over his father's death, must make adjustments to a move, a change in lifestyle, and entirely new feelings and emotions signifying adolescence. In addition to all this, Chris's grandfather dies. A helpful account not only of the loss of loved ones but of other changes occurring as a result and of how an adolescent learns to cope, recover courage, and discover new strength in the process of growing up.

Rawlings, M. K. *The yearling* (E. Shenton, Decorator). New York: Scribner's 1938. Fiction. Age 8 and over. Jody Baxter is the last surviving child of Ory and Penny Baxter. The Baxters live in Florida on a high rise of ground called Baxter's Island. Jody's only friend is a physically malformed young boy named Fodderwing. Life is difficult and death not far from most every door in the bush of Florida's interior during the time of the story; but Jody has not been personally touched, for his brothers and sisters died when he was very young and his mother does not permit animals as pets. For some time Jody has been unable to visit his sickly friend, Fodder-wing, because Jody's father has been bitten by a snake and Jody must help around the house. When Jody eventually gets to Fodder-wing's house, he is met by Buck, Fodder-wing's older brother, and told that Fodder-wing is dead. At first Jody cannot comprehend what is being said. Buck leads him to the room where Fodder-wing lies covered in a sheet up to his chin. Buck invites Jody to speak to the dead boy even though Fodder-wing would not hear him. Jody whispers "Hey," and when Fodder-wing does not answer, Jody understands that death is silence. Later, Jody's fawn, Flag, has to be killed because it is eating the crops and the family will starve unless something is done. All attempts to prevent Flag's destroying the crops fail, and Jody is devastated. During the terrible moment that Jody experiences in his grief over Flag, he compares Flag's death to that of Fodder-wing. Fodder-wing had died, and that was terrible; but the awfulness passed, and the awfulness of Flag's death would pass, too. But the knowledge that his father had gone "back on him," when he ordered the death of the fawn, is intolerable. Betrayal leaves no one to turn to in grief. Thus, the death of Flag becomes more difficult to bear. Eventually Jody and his dad become reconciled, and Jody emerges from all his pain with a more mature understanding of life and its purposes. This timeless classic is a must. It appeals to the young and not so young alike.

Rhodin, E. *The good greenwood.* Philadelphia: Westminster, 1972. Fiction. Age 12 and over. This tense and moving story is about Mike, who has lost his good friend Louie. Time passes slowly, but eventually Mike comes to realize that Louie is really dead and is not going to reappear around the next corner. Although he still grieves, he now begins to remember Louie for the clown and dreamer he was and for the good times they had together. These memories help him overcome his sorrow and pain. Good.

Roberts, J. *Emir's education in the proper use of magical powers* (L. Cherry & E. Friede, Illus.). New York: Delacorte, 1979. Fiction. Age 9 and over. Emir is a young prince who lives in a brand-new kingdom, with beautiful people, creatures, and plants—just about everything except seasons. People can live

forever if they want to, and they do not look old because
they do not know they are supposed to. Emir's father, the
king, decides to send Emir on a long journey around the
kingdom instead of sending him to school. He is to seek out
the land of the gods for answers to the problems of the
kingdom. Emir's journey is full of surprises. He invents the
first lie and finds that it is just as easy to invent truth. He
meets conscience and inspiration, leaves his body for the
first time, and invents the idea of death. This symbolic tale
contains an important message. The author says: "Emir is
that part of me and of everyone who at some time has to
question the meaning of life and death, and don't we each
think of ourselves as the center of our own kingdom as Emir
does?" A very unusual, creative, and effectively crafted story
that is deceptively simple. The meanings are profound.

Sanderlin, O. *Johnny.* Cranbury, N.J.: A. S. Barnes, 1968.
Nonfiction. Age 12 and over. A mother's account of her son,
who at the age of 11 is stricken with leukemia. The book
describes the boy's courageous struggle to lead a normal life
for almost five years until his death. A tribute to the
strength of the human spirit, especially in one so young.
Moving.

Schoen, B. *A place and a time.* New York: Crowell, 1967.
Fiction. Age 12 and over. This is a believable narrative of a
girl's nurturing family life and of her steadily growing
understanding of herself and others. Although death is not a
major theme in this story, it is nevertheless worth sharing in
Josie's reaction to and eventual acceptance of her beloved
grandmother's death. The loss, grief, and working through
are shown as an important part of the girl's growth to
maturity.

Shotter, R. *A matter of time.* New York: Collins & World,
1979. Fiction. Age 14 and over. In coping with grief, there
is an opportunity for self-discovery and the development of
a better sense of one's own identity. Lisl Gilbert is 16, and
her mother is dying of lung cancer. Lisl's mother had always
been the special person in the family—busy, vivacious, a
superstar. As she moves toward death, Lisl realizes that
behind all this activity her mother is insecure and lonely. In

one important moment, Lisl and her father are finally able to let her mother know that they do love her and that they know she loves them. By the time her mother dies—on the day of Lisl's high school graduation—Lisl has realized that she is free to use her own time to become a special person herself. Surprisingly for a book of this kind, a social worker appears as a prominent character who helps Lisl and her family to grow during these difficult few months.

Segerberg, O., Jr. *Living with death*. New York: Dutton, 1976. Nonfiction. Age 14 and over. The subject of death is discussed from anthropological, theological, historical, and thanatological perspectives. The author asks teen-agers to philosophize and probe. The coverage includes such topics as euthanasia, psychic research, North American views of death, attempts to avoid death through cryonics, and the work of Elisabeth Kübler-Ross. This is a broad survey of the subject of death. Informative, challenging.

Shotwell, L. R. *Adam Bookout*. New York: Viking, 1967. Fiction. Age 12 and over. Adam avoids acknowledging the deaths of his parents by pretending they are still alive. In his grief, he runs away from well-meaning guardians. When he reaches his destination, he meets a number of people from different backgrounds with many kinds of problems. He realizes that he is not the only one with problems. He learns, too, that problems are not left behind when people run away. Valuable.

Shreve, S. *Family secrets: Five very important stories* (R. Cuffari, Illus.). New York: Knopf, 1979. Fiction. Ages 7–9. In these five stories, eight-year-old Sammy tells about his experiences with the death of his dog, the divorce of his aunt and uncle, the suicide of his best friend's brother, his 70-year-old grandmother who has cancer and has recently moved in with Sammy's family, and cheating on a math test at school. Sammy's viewpoint is simple and insightful; he has the great advantage of sensitive and supportive parents.

Simon, N. *We remember Philip* (R. Sanderson, Illus.). Chicago: Whitman, 1979. Fiction. Ages 7–10. The text and pictures describe the responses of Sam and his classmates to the accidental death of their teacher's son, Philip. The children exchange feelings; and the class, with the help of the principal, offers support to the teacher as he works through his grief. The students urge their teacher to show pictures of Philip to the class, and the children plant a tree in his memory. Somewhat contrived and cool in tone.

Simon, S. *Life and death in nature.* New York: McGraw-Hill, 1976. Nonfiction. Ages 6–11. This is a valuable book. It deals with death from a scientific-experimental perspective. Experiments with earthworms grown and put into crowded or uncrowded environments to study their survival are described. The reader learns about decomposition, ecology, overpopulation, and the balance of nature. Although the book does not deal with the emotional aspects of the death of loved ones—people or pets—the young reader will not only be fascinated but perhaps comforted to discover that nutrients contained in living things today may once have been part of a rose petal, a dinosaur, or a human being of an earlier era. This recognition of the continuity of life is awe inspiring and may offer some reassurance at a time of loss. This book is instructive and causes the reader to reflect on the question of life and death and our part in it.

Slote, A. *Hang tough, Paul Mather.* Philadelphia: Lippincott, 1973. Fiction. Ages 9–12. Paul Mather, a sixth grader, loves baseball, and he is good at it, especially pitching. But Paul also has leukemia and is in his third remission when the story begins. His parents have moved twice, hoping to find the hospital that can cure their son. Now they have arrived in Michigan, and the Little League of baseball teams in the new neighborhood need Paul. He is needed as a pitcher for the Wilson Dairy team, and when his parents refuse to give permission until he has seen his new doctor, Paul fakes his parents' permission and plays anyway. His father is irate; his mother, frightened. Paul has trouble convincing his parents how much he needs to play baseball in order to keep up his hope. Paul's new doctor, Tom Kinsella, turns out to be of critical help. He is open, informal, understanding, and becomes personally involved. When Paul is hospitalized, he visits three or four times a day. Twice, when Paul had vomited, he helped the orderly clean up. But most of all, in

Paul's own words, "He knew how to break bad news better than any doctor I ever had." In this deeply moving book, the author tells of the courageous struggle of a young boy to cope with his illness, with his parents' protectiveness, and eventually with the knowledge that he has little time left to live. The author has an uncanny ability to evoke emotions by a style of writing that is full of understatements and has a simplicity that speaks eloquently. Inspiring.

Smith, D. B. *A taste of blackberries.* New York: Crowell, 1973. Fiction. Preschool to 6. A little boy is confronted with loss, grief, and guilt when his best friend, Jamie, dies from being stung by a bee while the two are picking blackberries. The feeling of guilt is natural enough. Jamie had a way of kidding around, so that, when he rolled on the ground after the bee sting, his friend thought he was only joking. After a time, the boy comes to accept his friend's death. The story is simply and sensitively written and richly illustrated. The book won a Child Study Association award.

Sperry, A. *Call it courage.* New York: Macmillan, 1956. Fiction. Ages 10–14. This is the story of "Mafatu, the Boy Who Was Afraid," who lived on a South Sea Island and battled with Moana, the Sea God, for a peaceful existence with the sea. Mafatu wins the battle with his own fear of the sea, which he projects onto the sea god. As the story goes, Mafatu was three when he and his mother were caught by a hurricane while on a reef fishing for sea urchins. As the winds and rain beat on the canoe, it capsized, so the child held on to his mother as she tried to swim to the shore of Tekoto, an uninhabited islet. Sharks circled them at one point, and the boy sensed that Moana was reaching up to pull them down into the sea. They made shore, but the mother died after pressing some coconut meat to her weakened child's lips. The boy's father, who was the island chief, had named him Mafatu—Stout Heart—but this incident created such fear of the sea in Mafatu that he was ridiculed. The other boys his age excluded him from their games. The girls laughed, for what kind of husband would he make, afraid, as he was, of the sea by which they all lived. The older people blamed the ghost spirit. When Mafatu is an adolescent, he slips away one night in a canoe to "do battle with the sea"—his fear. He finds himself on an uninhabited island that is visited periodically by headhunters; and during this time, he becomes a man, conquers his fear, builds a canoe, and sails back to his island, where he collapses in his proud father's arms. A highly readable book of adventure, fear and courage, life, and death.

Stein, S. B. *About dying.* New York: Walker, 1974. Fiction. Preschool to 9. This sensitively written book is designed for both children and parents, with separate texts for each group. Vivid photographs accompany the children's texts, which deal with the death of Snow, a pet bird, and with Eric's, Michael's, and Jane's grandfather. The children have a funeral for Snow and participate in their grandpa's funeral. The parents' text serves as a resource for handling the children's questions. Death is dealt with in an honest and straightforward, but low-keyed, manner and with deep sensitivity.

Stevens, M. *When Grandpa died.* (K. Ualand, Photographer). Chicago: Childrens Press, 1979. Fiction. Preschool to 7. Fourteen brightly colored and strikingly beautiful photographs face pages with a brief first-person narrative text telling about a little girl's relationship with her grandfather, his assistance in helping her to talk about death and to bury a dead bird that they found, and her efforts (with help from her parents) to cope with his illness and subsequent death. A simple story, directly told.

Stolz, M. *By the highway home.* New York: Harper, 1971. Fiction. Age 12 and up. When her brother Beau is killed in Vietnam, 13-year-old Catty and her family are dejected. Only after her father loses his engineering job and her family moves halfway across the nation to help run a family inn, do its members begin to come to terms with their loss. For the family, going on with life without regrets and self-recriminations is a major achievement. The characters are realistically drawn.

Stolz, M. *The edge of next year.* New York: Harper, 1974. Fiction. Ages 11–14. Orin and Vic Woodward are in the family car when the accident in which their mother is killed happens. Orin, 14, takes on the housework, the care of his younger brother, and the worry about his father, who tries to drown his grief by drinking. The story graphically describes both the shock and pain the mother's death causes the family and the problem of alcoholism. Eventually the father joins Alcoholics Anonymous, thus providing a hopeful note. This is a gripping and realistic story.

Stull, E. G. *My turtle died today*. New York: Holt, 1964. Preschool to 8. When Boxer, a little boy's pet turtle, dies, the boy and his friends have a funeral and get into a discussion of the meaning of being alive and dead. As the children look at new kittens, they realize that "they have to live first before they die." The story is rather contrived and didactic. Despite this shortcoming, the concepts of life and death are presented in a simple and understandable manner.

Talbot, T. *Dear Greta Garbo*. New York: Putnam's, 1978. Fiction. Ages 12–14. Thirteen-year-old Miranda and her grandmother are both stricken by the sudden death of her grandfather. When Grandma moves into the bedroom in their New York City apartment that Miranda was to have inherited from her older college-bound sister, both of their lives are further disturbed, and each finds herself at a crossroads. The two console and support each other, but it is only when they are again able to assert their independence— Grandma by taking a job as a part-time cashier at the movie theater and moving back to her own apartment, and Miranda by cutting her hair short in the style of Greta Garbo—that they begin to recover and to be able to help Miranda's mother deal with her own grief. A well-told tale of cross-generational similarities in grief and growth.

Thomas, I. *Hi, Mrs. Mallory!* (A. Toulmin-Rothe, Illus.). New York: Harper, 1979. Fiction. Ages 6–8. A young black girl, Li'l Bits, describes her special friendship with her neighbor, Mrs. Mallory. They share fun and fantasy together, but one day Mrs. Mallory is no longer home. She is dead and Li'l Bits is sad, though Mrs. Mallory's dog comes to live with her. The death is abrupt and unexplained; its consequences are not as well developed as is the predeath relationship.

Tobias, T. *Petey*. (S. Shimin, Illus.). New York: Putnam's, 1978.

Fiction. Ages 7–9. Emily is a little girl who has a pet gerbil named Petey. One day when she comes home from school, Emily finds Petey sick. By the next morning he is dead. This is a first-person narrative interspersed with memory flashbacks. The author very capably helps the reader empathize with Emily's feelings of anger, sadness, and love as she grieves her pet's death and comes to accept her loss. The story is warm and sensitive, as are the drawings.

Tolan, S. S. *Grandpa—and me.* New York: Scribner's, 1978. Fiction. Ages 9–14. In this first-person narrative, 11-year-old Kerry Warren tells how she, her older brother Matt, and her parents are trying to cope with her 80-year-old grandfather's senility. The account is given from the perspective of a mature, loving, and caring granddaughter. It does not spare the reader the troublesome, embarrassing, and painful details of her grandfather's confusion, loss of memory, and loss of bodily functions. The family's routine is disrupted; Grandpa needs constant supervision. At a family meeting they discuss whether to place Grandpa in a nursing home. The children rebel at the thought of such an arrangement. During brief periods of lucidity, Grandpa is frustratingly aware of his condition. Then early one morning he packs his things in boxes, marks them for family members, walks to the park, and drowns himself in the swimming pool. This story is gripping; the problems with which it deals are realistic; and its style is straightforward and unsentimental. A must.

Tresselt, A. *The dead tree* (C. Robins, Illus.). New York: Parents' Magazine Press, 1972. Fiction. Preschool to 7. This unusual book depicts poetically and through illustration the life cycle of an oak tree. Death is portrayed as a natural and necessary part of this life cycle. It is shown that in nature nothing is ever wasted and nothing completely dies—a hopeful message for the young reader. Instructive.

Turner, A. *Houses for the dead: Burial customs through the ages.* New York: McKay, 1976. Nonfiction. Age 12 and over. This book presents a carefully researched history of burial customs, funeral vehicles, exposure of bodies, scavengers, and the like. Sometimes a case history is told at length; at other times, the work jumps from culture to culture, from century to century, to make a point. In this respect, the book is somewhat uneven. The author's descriptions are vivid. Included is rich material about loss and how the beliefs of various cultural groups affect their rituals.

Uchida, Y. *The birthday visitor.* New York: Scribner's, 1975. Fiction. Ages 7-9. This beautiful story is about Emi, a Japanese-American girl, and what happens at her birthday party. A baby sparrow has fallen from the nest on Emi's birthday. The birthday celebration includes a funeral for the dead bird and a burial under a peach tree. A Japanese minister is the birthday visitor after whom the book is titled. The language is simple and direct, and characters and events are vividly portrayed.

Viorst, J. *The tenth good thing about Barney.* New York: Atheneum, 1971. Fiction. Ages 5-9. When the little boy's cat, Barney, dies, his mother helps him prepare for the funeral and offers comfort by asking the boy to think of 10 good things about Barney. He can only think of 9. But with the help of his father he is able to add the 10th good thing: "Barney is in the ground and he's helping grow flowers." Although many very young children may not understand the concept of Barney's role as fertilizer, the language is generally simple and concrete. The story is gentle and hopeful and portrays parents who are deeply sensitive to children's needs and capable of giving them comfort.

Vogel, I. M. *My twin sister, Erika.* New York: Harper, 1976. Fiction. Ages 6-9. This is the story of Erika and Inge, who are identical twins. Inge is jealous of her exuberant and more creative twin sister and often tells her that she hates her and wishes she were dead. Erika, too, sometimes wishes her twin, Inge, were dead. Erika bosses Inge because she is the "big" sister—older by 30 minutes. Both jealously outdo themselves in their friendship with Magda next door. Then one day Erika becomes feverish and is put to bed. At first Inge enjoys her status of being the one up and about. She even feels more loved when her bed is moved into her parents' bedroom. But Erika is very sick and one night she dies. Inge's parents tell her, "You are the only one now." The story very perceptively deals with the special identity problems that identical

twins often have and how important it is for parents to be
alert and to help twins achieve a sense of uniqueness. The
death of the twin sister in this story causes special problems
for Inge. At first, having been so closely identified with
Erika, she feels like only the part "left over," until she
begins to develop her own separate identity and realize that
she is loved. Inge also has to overcome her strong feelings of
guilt about having wished her sister dead and her fear that
perhaps she, through the magic power of her wish, actually
brought about her twin's death. A young reader might
falsely assume that the death of an identical twin can
facilitate the other's independence. With parental guidance,
this book is recommended. Most young readers who have
siblings can relate well to the problems of jealousy, which
are realistically portrayed. The black-and-white drawings are
highly appealing and sensitive.

Walker, M. *Year of the cafeteria.* Indianapolis: Bobbs-Merrill,
1971. Fiction. Age 12 and over. This is a first-person
narrative that skillfully portrays the development of a warm,
if complex, relationship between a teen-age girl and her
grandmother. When her grandmother dies, she refuses to
believe it until she hears the principal of the school where
Grandma had worked announce the sad news to the students. Now the girl is no longer able to turn to her grandma
for help and companionship. The girl's grief and mourning
are sympthetically, sensitively, and realistically described.

Warburg, S. *Growing time.* Boston: Houghton Mifflin, 1969.
Fiction. Ages 7–10. The central character in this story is
Jamie, whose old dog King dies, leaving the boy lonely,
angry, and sad. His parents rush to replace King with a new
puppy, which Jamie rejects at first. Different family members explain to the little boy what happened to King after
he died. An uncle tells Jamie that King's body becomes part
of the rich earth that feeds us. Grandmother talks about
King's spirit that never dies because it is stored in a loving
heart. Jamie is comforted and accepts his puppy when he
recognizes how helpless and in need of care the puppy is.
The story is carefully crafted and vividly and beautifully
written. It offers comfort as well as information about the
finality of physical death.

Watts, R. G. *Straight talk about death with young people.* Philadelphia: Westminster, 1975. Nonfiction. Ages 12 and over. Aimed toward helping young people, this book grew out of the author's experience in discussion groups with seventh and eighth graders. It explores facts and feelings about death and dying, grief, funerals, and hopes by which people live and die. A frank and honest book that avoids romanticizing and minimizing issues, facts, and feelings.

Wersba, G. *The dream watcher.* New York: Atheneum, 1968. Fiction. Age 12 and over. Albert's entire life has seemed empty, and his relationship with his family has not been good. Then he meets Mrs. Woodfin, an eccentric old lady who encourages Albert to see himself as an acceptable, interesting human being. She tells Albert that she had been a famous actress when she was young, but when she realized that fame and fortune do not bring happiness, she gave up acting. Unexpectedly, Mrs. Woodfin dies of a heart attack. Albert learns that she had been a lonely old woman on welfare who had never been able to hold a job because she drank too much. At first he is angered, but when he remembers all she has meant to him, he continues to cherish her in his memories.

Wersba, B. *Run softly, go fast.* New York: Atheneum, 1970. Fiction. Age 16 and over. David Marks, 19, has just returned home from his father's funeral. He hates his father and decides to write a journal about their relationship. He remembers that when he was young his father was the most important person in his life. Slowly, his feelings had changed. This may have started when Dave discovered that his dad was having an affair with another woman; it may have been a reaction to his father's dislike of Dave's poetry and paintings; or it may have been when Dave realized what a ruthless businessman his father was. The final break came when his father accused Dave's best friend of "being a queer." Dave then moved out of the house to live in the "hip" community. He rarely spoke to his father. When his father was in the hospital dying of cancer, Dave came to visit him, however. Nearing the end of the journal, Dave recognizes errors in his recollections, gains a new perspective, and is able to perceive his father differently. A believable story to which young people can relate well. It deals with the difficulties adolescents and youths have in accepting their parents as human beings with faults. Writing a journal helped David resolve his anger and facilitated his grieving for his father.

White, E. B. *Charlotte's web.* New York: Harper, 1952. Fiction. Ages 8–11. This beautiful and popular story is about Wilber, a pig; Templeton, a rat; and their friendship with Charlotte, a spider. Charlotte's death and the subsequent rebirth of her children help explain how the cycle of life continues through children. The story also describes the grief and sorrow one experiences after the death of a close friend and shows how memories of a dead friend can be kept alive in a healthy manner. A classic.

Whitehead, R. *The mother tree.* New York: Seabury, 1971. Fiction. Ages 8–12. When Tempe's mother dies suddenly, the 10-year-old girl quite suddenly has to take care of her 4-year-old sister Laurie and help with the household chores. To make matters worse, Laurie continually asks, "When will Mother come back?" Tempe's own impulses to play and be free of this burden of responsibility make her feel guilty. But the patience and kindness Tempe shows toward her little sister help Laurie to face the fact that her mother is dead and cannot return. At the end of a long summer, Tempe is rewarded by her father's praise and gratitude. This is a moving story.

Winthrop, E. *Walking away.* New York: Harper, 1973. Fiction. Age 11 and over. Emily has come to spend another summer with her grandparents on their farm, a place she loves to visit, a world that does not change. Emily and her grandfather are especially close and have many serious talks about people and situations, and about death. After Grandpa injures himself, Emily finds that the farm is not well kept, and this disturbs her greatly. When Nina, her friend, comes to visit, Emily's loyalties are torn between her unpredictable friend and her steady grandfather. Grandpa dies that winter, but Emily remembers their talks and is comforted by this memory. Well written, with an easy flow of dialogue and sensitive portrayal of life, death, and changing relationships.

Woodford, P. *Please don't go.* New York: Dutton, 1972. Fiction. Age 14 and over. This is a story about a 15-year-old English girl who, after spending her summer vacation in France, faces the many problems of growing up—problems of self-acceptance, keeping a friendship with a girl friend whose personality tends to drive people away, infatuation with an "older man," and finally the problem of accepting the death of a young man of whom she has grown fond. A sensitive story.

Young, J. *When the whale came to my town* (D. Bernstein, Photographer). New York: Knopf, 1974. Fiction. Ages 6–12. This is a moving account of a boy's encounter with a whale who has beached itself at the tip of Cape Cod. The boy stays with the dying whale for three days while other children, townspeople, sailors, the coast guard, and several doctors come and go. All efforts fail to persuade the whale to go back into the water. The boy, sitting with the whale late into the night, is awed and forced to ponder the question of life and death. The photographs add vividness to the story, which is based on the author's personal experience. Powerful and tender.

Zim, H., and Bleeker, S. *Life and death.* New York: Morrow, 1970. Nonfiction. Age 9 and over. In this pioneering book the authors discuss in plain language the biologic, physical, and chemical facts of life and death and the naturalness of the life cycle for plants, animals, and humans. In addition, the authors deal with people's attitudes toward death and with various death and funeral customs in different cultures; they bring the reader up to our present best definition and determination of medical death. This is a scientific and dispassionate account, yet not at all insensitive. What impresses most is that this little book contains a great many of the answers to children's questions about death that often are not available to them through interaction with adults. This information-packed volume is most valuable because it will help in avoiding misconceptions and fantasies about aspects of death that are unpleasant and distasteful to many adults. The book has a hopeful conclusion: it suggests that people who lead useful and happy lives are likely to come to an acceptance of all life, including its end. Outstanding.

Zindel, B., & Zindel, P. *A star for the latecomer.* New York: Harper, 1980. Fiction. Age 12 and over. Brooke Hillary is 17 and lives on Long Island, but she commutes into New York City to attend a school for youngsters seeking a theatrical career. Her mother—who is 46 and has advanced bone cancer—wants Brooke to be something special, and Brooke tries hard to become a star before her mother dies. For herself, Brooke likes dancing, but she really would rather just have a boy friend and be like other girls. This could have been little more than a tale of intergenerational conflict, but the authors know that real life is more complex than that. Mother and daughter do love each other, but each must seek her own freedom and fulfillment.

Zindel, P. *The pigman.* New York: Harper, 1968. Fiction. Age 12 and over. This is a moving story about two young people who come from homes where love is largely absent. They pursue a destructive course, caring little for anyone but themselves, finding excuses for their behavior, and blaming others for their own ineptitudes. When their friend, Mr. Pignanti, nicknamed Mr. Pigman, dies, however, they finally recognize the tragic consequences of their behavior. The story ends leaving the impression that Mr. Pigman's death and its irreversibility will bring about positive changes in the young people's behavior.

Zolotow, C. *My grandson Lew.* (W. Pene Du Bois, Illus.). New York: Harper, 1974. Fiction. Preschool to 8. Four years have passed since Grandfather died. Now Lewis is six and suddenly tells his mother that he misses his grandfather. His mother had assumed Lewis had been too young to remember his grandfather. Now, to her surprise, she finds that Lewis remembers many experiences with great clarity, such as the scratchy beard when Grandpa kissed him, the time he took him to the place that had many pictures to look at, and the time Grandpa let him warm his hand around the pipe. Lewis confides to his mother that he has missed Grandpa and has been waiting for him to return. Lewis's mother, in turn, tells the little boy that she has missed him, too. Sharing their memories of Grandpa make Lewis and his mother a little less sad. This story, a work of art in which each sentence is written with restraint and charm, provides evidence of the author's deep insight into the world of a child. Du Bois's pictures are vivid and project the same kind of warmth and love that characterize the text.

AUDIOVISUAL RESOURCES

RICHARD A. PACHOLSKI

Presented here is the most thorough mediography to date on children and death, a collection of 143 annotated items. The entries are numbered for convenience in using the topical index on p. 187, and are arranged alphabetically by title. Initials following the title suggest audiences for which the item would be appropriate:

GS: grade school
MS: middle school
HS: high school
A: adults—general audiences, undergraduates, and professionals in training
P: professionals with specialized interests

Following the discussion of the content of the item is the name of a distributor and other factual information such as kind of medium (film, videotape, filmstrip, audiocassette), running time, and release or publication date if known.

Distributor identification and addresses given have been checked and rechecked against all current directories and catalogs, but users of audiovisuals should be alert to unexpected changes. It is important to realize, too, that in most cases the distributor listed for each item is not the only one handling the item; it is simply the one we have used or have seen advertised nationally. Users of audiovisuals should be alert to distributors or other sources of media in their own areas or communities and should remember that not-for-profit media libraries—in medical schools, colleges and universities, clinics, hospitals, public

153

libraries, schools, churches, or funeral homes—often make materials available for substantially lower cost than do commerical distributors. In addition, organizations like the American Cancer Society, Leukemia Society of America, National Association for Mental Health, and National Sudden Infant Death Syndrome Foundation maintain large audiovisual collections, especially in topics of interest, and should be consulted. Write for catalogs of available audiovisuals and ask to be put on mailing lists for information about new releases.

I have decided not to include the rental or purchase prices and terms of audiovisual materials because such information changes rapidly. If one is operating on a limited budget, one must double check with the distributor in any event and must be sure to search out alternative sources of supply, perhaps with the aid of librarians or media specialists. Users certainly can save money on audiovisuals by combining careful consideration of alternative media on a given topic with a judicious search for and selection of distributors. I recently taught a four-week course using 23 films and videotapes, all critically acclaimed, available from four local sources. The only expense involved was return postage for eight of the items.

A topical index to this chapter is located on page 187. Topics and subtopics in the area of children and death are suggested and annotated; then the numbers of relevant audiovisual items are listed under each heading. Many audiovisuals, of course, appear in several categories. Teachers and others searching for appropriate materials should find the index a helpful tool in making their choices.

For information on additional audiovisuals and other resources on all death and dying topics, refer to H. Wass, C. A. Corr, R. A. Pacholski, & C. M. Sanders, *Death education: An annotated resource guide,* Washington: Hemisphere, 1980. See also H. Wass & C. A. Corr (Eds.), *Childhood and death,* Washington: Hemisphere, in press.

List of Audiovisuals

1. *Adolescent Suicide: A Documentary* (A). Dr. Herman Farberow and other staff members at the Suicide Prevention

Center in Los Angeles discuss factors in the alarmingly high rate of adolescent suicide, the effects on survivors, and possible methods of prevention and intervention. Included are interviews with youths who have attempted suicide. The Charles Press, Bowie, MD 20715; audiocassette, 54 minutes; 1973.

2. *After Our Baby Died: Sudden Infant Death Syndrome* (A). This well-made, impressive film, winner of a blue ribbon in mental health at the 1976 American Film Festival, was created to help professionals and others who come in contact with SIDS parents to understand the syndrome better. Parents are interviewed and offer telling lessons and insights for care givers. Free loan from the National SIDS Foundation, Room 1904, 310 S. Michigan Ave., Chicago, IL 60604; color; 20 minutes; 1976. Write the foundation for information on several other audiovisuals available.

3. *All the Way Home* (HS, A). The novel on which this fine film is based, *A Death in the Family,* is one of the most profoundly moving, most searching, and best written analyses of family reactions to the death of a member in all literature. Particularly important are the many cameo portraits of grief: the dead man's wife, his two very young children, and various other relatives. Religious belief—or lack of it—as a conditioning factor in responding to death is studied in minute detail. The novel is essential reading for everyone trying to understand death, and the film also makes a major contribution. Films, Inc., 1144 Wilmette Ave., Wilmette, IL 60091; black and white; 103 minutes; 1963.

4. *American Association of Suicidology, Proceedings of the Conference, 1978: A Set of Presentations on Adolescent Suicide* (P). Titles include "Suicide and Children," "Suicide Methods and Potential in Ages 4-12," "Intent and Death Attitudes of Adolescents," and "Mobilizing Help in Adolescent Suicide," Highly Specialized Promotions, 391 Atlantic Ave., Brooklyn, NY 11201; four audiocassettes.

5. *American Cancer Society, National Conference on Childhood Cancer: Meeting Highlights* (A, P). American Cancer Society, 777 Third Ave., New York, NY 10017; film; 2 hours; 1974.

6. *And We Were Sad, Remember?* (HS, A). In a 2-minute dramatized episode, a small family group (mother, father, and two young children) reacts to Grandmother's death. Then there is a 10-minute discussion involving various children and adults about what it is like to lose a parent. The major point made is that it is not easy but that children must always know the truth. This well-made and informative program is one of a series called "Footsteps," sponsored by the U.S. Office of Education, on approaches to parenting. A viewer's guide to the whole series may be obtained from Consumer Information Center, Pueblo, CO 81009. The film is available from the National Audiovisual Center, Order Section, Washington, D.C. 20409; color; 30 minutes.

7. *Anna and Poppy* (A). Faced with the death of her grandfather, Poppy, young Anna comes to learn that memories of shared love and happy times together can overcome the effects of sadness. This film can foster discussion and sensitize audiences to death in the family and to the nature and function of the bonds of love. University of Illinois, Visual Aids Service, 1325 S. Oak St., Champaign, IL 61820; color; 15 minutes; 1977.

8. *Annie and The Old One* (GS, HS). Annie, a Navajo girl, loves her grandmother, the Old One, very much. When the grandmother tells Annie she expects to "return to the earth" when a new rug she is weaving is taken from the loom, Annie tries to delay its completion. Based on a book by Miska Miles, the film is a beautiful portrayal of death and the meaning of the generations from a child's point of view. University of Illinois, Visual Aids Service, 1325 S. Oak St., Champaign, IL 61820; color; 16 minutes; 1976.

9. *But Jack was a Good Driver* (HS, A). His schoolmates begin to suspect that Jack's death in an auto accident may have been a suicide. Subsequent discussion shows the students considering their own attitude toward suicide, dispels some myths, presents the warning signs to look for, and offers suggestions on relating to and working with suicidal people. University of California at Berkeley, Extension Media Center, 2223 Fulton St., Berkeley, CA 94720; color film; 15 minutes; 1974.

10. *A Call for Help* (A). This is a training film for police officers, rescue workers, and emergency room personnel, although a general range of care givers will find it valuable. Specific lessons are offered for dealing with cases of SIDS. A study guide is available. Free loan from National SIDS Foundation, Room 1904, 310 S. Michigan Ave., Chicago, IL 60604; color; 20 minutes; 1976.

11. *Chickamauga* (HS, A). Based on the Ambrose Bierce short story, the film graphically portrays the terror and the folly of war from the perspective of a six-year-old deaf mute. Viewfinders, Inc., Box 1665, Evanston, IL 60204; black and white; 33 minutes.

12. *Childhood Cancer: Emotional Effects* (P). This videotape is available for medical professionals. M. D. Anderson Hospital and Tumor Institute, Medical Communications Department, University of Texas System Cancer Center, Houston, TX 77025; color; 58 minutes, 1975.

13. *Children and Death* (A). When children experience the death of someone close, their special needs demand knowledgeable and honest intervention. The topic is explored with an audience of parents, teachers, counselors, medical personnel, and clergy in mind. Wolfelt Productions, 814 W. Charles St., Muncie, IN 47305; color filmstrip (or slides) and audio-cassette; discussion manual; 15 minutes; 1979.

14. *Children and Death* (A). Included in this program are discussions about children's experiences with death, their perceptions and questions about it, and a series of related suggestions for adults. J. A. B. Press, Box 213-J, Fairlawn, NJ 07410; three audiocassettes.

15. *Children and Death* (A). Dr. Simon Yudkin gives an overview of essential aspects of this topic: the importance of death education for children, the significance of religious training, and the need to allow children to participate in death rituals and mourning. Communications in Learning, 2280 Main St., Buffalo, NY 14214; audiocassette; 40 minutes.

16. *Children and Death: A Guide for Parents and Teachers* (A). This program provides general answers to a number of questions: How does one tell a child about death? What should one say and not say? What form should death

education take, and when? Should children be allowed to attend funerals? Allied Memorial Council, P.O. Box 30112, Seattle, WA 98103; audiocassette; teacher's guide. See also *Understanding Death Series.*

17. *Children and Dying Conference, University of Chicago, 1977: Proceedings* (A, P). Audiocassettes are available on these topics: "Care for the Caregivers," "The Child and Sudden Death," "What Shall We Tell the Children?," "The Dying Child at Home," "The Dying Child in the Hospital," and "Parental Loss and Childhood Bereavement." Highly Specialized Promotions, 391 Atlantic Ave., Brooklyn, NY 11201; available as a set or individually.

18. *Children Die Too* (P). See *Physician's Role with the Dying Patient.*

19. *Children in Crisis: Death* (A). The titles of the five filmstrips in this series accurately suggest the content: "Death as a Reality of Life," "Expressing Grief," "Ages of Understanding," "Explaining Death to Children," and "The Importance of Funerals." Reviewers (for example, *Death Education,* 1977, *1,* 351–353) suggest the program may have value for general audiences or beginning death educators but lacks depth. Parent's Magazine Films, Dept. F, 52 Vanderbilt Ave., New York, NY 10017; color, with audiocassettes or record; scripts and discussion guide.

20. *Children's Conceptions of Death* (A, P). This critically acclaimed program is well organized and informative. Children at various ages—under 5, between 6 and 9, and 10 and older—have different and developing attitudes toward death and differing needs in the face of it. Teachers, care givers, and parents will find these lessons most helpful. University of Wisconsin-Milwaukee, School of Nursing, Box 413, Milwaukee, WI 53201; color videotape; 40 minutes; teacher's guide: 1974.

21. *A Child's Eyes: November 22, 1963* (A). This short film provides valuable insights into the minds of children and into basic human questions of life and death. A number of five- and six-year-olds react to the assassination of President Kennedy through crayon drawings and their own narrative. Julian Morris Agency, 1350 Avenue of the Americas, New York, NY 10019; color; 9 minutes.

22. *Cipher in the Snow* (HS, A). This excellent film tells a moving story of a school boy's sudden and unexplained death and how he had been written off as a zero (or so he felt) by his parents, classmates, and teachers, none of whom, as they realize after the fact, really knew the boy. Is it possible to die physically as well as emotionally from lack of love? Saying yes in a convincing but not maudlin way, the film could trigger discussion of the essential relationship between love and life. Brigham Young University, DMDP Media Business Services, W 164 Stadium, Provo, UT 84602; color; 25 minutes; 1974.

23. *A Conference on the Dying Child* (P). A pediatric head nurse, a nursing supervisor, and a nursing instructor share their experiences and opinions about working with dying children. Emotions are a major issue, for nurse and family alike. Also discussed are children's concepts of death and their origins; how nurses should respond in given situations; and how, when, and whether the truth should be told. American Journal of Nursing Company, 267 W. 25th St., New York, NY 10001; film or videotape; black and white; 44 minutes; 1967.

24. *Coping* (A). This film documents a series of interviews between a doctor, a young boy terminally ill with leukemia, and his parents. What is remarkable about the boy and his family is the level of acceptance of the disease and of death that they have reached together; they understand the prognosis and discuss it openly and honestly. The film demonstrates the great value of healthy familial relationships when someone is dying. University of California at Berkeley, Extension Media Center, 2223 Fulton St., Berkeley, CA 94720; 22 minutes; 1974.

25. *Coping with Death and Dying: Emotional Needs of the Dying Patient and the Family* (A). Here perhaps is the "essential Kübler-Ross," at least in audiocassette format. This 180-minute tape series is certainly the longest and most detailed presentation of her views outside of her writing and follows the format of argument and explanation familiar to readers of *On Death and Dying*. On Tape 1, "The Fear of Death: Verbal and Nonverbal Symbolical Language," Küb-

ler-Ross reports how her research began and the early
distrust and hostility of her medical colleagues. Then she
explains that many patients see death as an impersonal,
catastrophic force and that care givers should be able to
pick up on verbal and nonverbal expressions of these
attitudes and feelings. Clinical examples are used to illustrate. Tapes 2 and 3 present the now-familiar stages of
dying in considerable detail and with a wealth of illustrative
case studies. Children and death is the topic of Tape 4.
Again citing case studies, Kübler-Ross treats the basic concerns of truth telling, problems caused by denying parents,
helping parents cope, children's conceptions of death, and
how these conceptions develop during the process of dying.
On Tape 5, sudden death is discussed from the viewpoint of
emergency room personnel. How does one tell the waiting
survivors or others injured in the same accident? How does
one give such information on the telephone? Should emotional outpouring be encouraged? Do survivors need to see
the body? What of the emotional needs of medical professionals, after their efforts have failed? Highly Specialized
Promotions, 391 Atlantic Ave., Brooklyn, NY 11201; five
audiocassettes; 30 minutes each; 1973.

26. *Counseling the Terminally Ill* (A, P). Medical care givers are
the primary audience for this detailed film introduction to
the physical and psychological needs of dying patients, both
adults and children, in the clinical setting. The emphasis is
on effective communication on matters of diagnosis, prognosis, treatment regimen, and involvement of family members. Write Charles A. Garfield, Ph.D., 106 Evergreen Lane,
Berkeley, CA 94705; color; 55 minutes.

27. *Crib Death: Or Sudden Infant Death Syndrome* (P). This is
a videotaped lecture by a physician, Barbara Bruner. Georgia
Regional Medical Television Network, Emory University
School of Medicine, 69 Butler St. S.E., Atlanta, GA 30303;
black and white; 47 minutes; 1972.

28. *Crib Death: Sudden Infant Death Syndrome* (A). In this
round-table discussion, Dr. John Coe reviews current research and statistics on SIDS. Nurse Carolyn Szybist and
parents who have lost children to SIDS discuss their bad

experiences—the fears, the guilt, the ignorance of outsiders—as well as great benefits offered by the National SIDS Foundation and its self-help activities. Additional suggestions for care givers are offered. The Charles Press, Bowie, MD 20715; audiocassette; 59 minutes; 1972.

29. *Crisis: The Hospitalized Child* (A). A chaplain, a 16-year-old cystic fibrosis patient, and her family discuss the disease, treatment methods, and the inevitable outcome. Communications in Learning, 2280 Main St., Buffalo, NY 14214; audiocassette, 37 minutes.

30. *A Cry for the Children* (HS, A). This short film has much to offer: insights into the effects on fire fighters of witnessing the deaths of children in fires; chilling warnings of the lethal nature of house fires; information about fire awareness and prevention; and, focusing on children, reminders of what life is all about. A fine film to trigger discussion, well made and fast paced. Film Communicators, 11136 Weddington St., Hollywood, CA 91601; color; 11 minutes; 1977.

31. *The Day Grandpa Died* (HS, A). David comes home from school one afternoon and is told that his beloved grandfather has died. "I don't want Grandpa dead," he cries. Then his mind gradually fills with happy memories of shared experiences. David's father is particularly helpful and understanding: "You've lost your grandpa and your friend, but I've lost my father," beautifully making an essential point about generations. The graveside ceremony helps David come to terms with the fact of the death so he can resume living, rich in his memories. University of California at Berkeley, Extension Media Center, 2223 Fulton St., Berkeley, CA 94720; color film; 12 minutes; 1970.

32. *A Day in the Death of Donnie B* (A). Donnie B. is a young inner-city drug addict, and his death at the end of a short, miserable life is a foregone conclusion. Voice-over commentary on the drug problem by mothers, doctors, police officers, ex-addicts, and members of the clergy adds chilling irony to the reality of Donnie's dying. National Institute of Mental Health, Drug Abuse Film Collection, National Audiovisual Center, General Services Administration, Washington, D.C. 20409; black-and-white film; 18 minutes.

33. *The Dead Bird* (GS, HS, A). Cartoon pictures and voice-over narration tell the Margaret Wise Brown story of a group of children who discover, bury, and mourn a dead bird. There are insights here into children's attitudes toward death. Indiana University, Audio-Visual Center, Bloomington, IN 47401; color film; 13 minutes; 1972.

34. *Dealing with Loss and Grief* (A, P). See *Death and Dying: Closing the Circle.*

35. *Dear Little Lightbird* (A). The subject, an incurably ill "blue baby," is the three-year-old son of the film maker. Viewfinders, Inc., Box 1665, Evanston, IL 60204; color; 19 minutes.

36. *Death—A Natural Part of Living* (GS). In addition to making the key point referred to in the title, this program surveys a variety of contemporary death-related issues and examines attitudes toward death in other lands and at other times. Marsh Film Enterprises, P.O. Box 8082, Shawnee Mission, KS 66208; filmstrip (65 frames) and audiocassette or record; teacher's guide; 1977.

37. *Death and Dying: Closing the Circle* (A, P). This extensive introductory program on death and dying consists of five color filmstrips, with accompanying audiocassettes or records and a discussion guide and study outline. Consultants are Robert Jay Lifton, M.D., and Professor Austin H. Kutscher. In Part 1, "The Meaning of Death," Lifton surveys death in our society. Part 2, "A Time to Mourn, a Time To Choose," examines death, burial, and memorial rites and society's underlying beliefs, assumptions, and attitudes about them. In Part 3, "Walk in the World for Me," Doris Lund retells her son Eric's five-year struggle with leukemia. Part 4, "Dealing with the Critically Ill Patient," features an interview with a man with cardiovascular disease. He relates his reaction to his disease, and suggestions are offered for care givers working with high-risk patients. Part 5, "Dealing with Loss and Grief," consisting of interviews with survivors of a young cancer victim, provides commentary and analysis of the nature of grief. This set of programs is one of the better introductory surveys in the field. Guidance Associates, Communications Park, Box 300, White Plains, NY 10603.

38. *Death and Dying: When a Child Dies* (A, P). Dr. C. Charles Bachmann interviews a mother who has lost several of her children to a genetic disease. Communications in Learning, 2280 Main St., Buffalo, NY 14214; audiocassette; 43 minutes.

39. *Death and the Child* (A). Dr. Edgar Jackson tells parents, health professionals, and teachers to be honest, truthful, and realistic in teaching children about death, in answering their questions, and in helping them through death crises. Anything less can cause emotional problems. Specific approaches, resources, and skills are suggested. The Charles Press, Bowie, MD 20715; audiocassette; 45 minutes; 1972.

40. *Death and the Family: From the Caring Professions' Point of View* (A, P). Professor Delphie Fredlund lectures on effective treatment of dying children and on the preparation and responsibilities of care givers of the dying. The Charles Press, Bowie, MD 20715; audiocassette; 30 minutes; 1972.

41. *Death Be not Proud* (HS, A). This is a film version of John Gunther's famous 1949 memoir of the dying and death of his 17-year-old son, victim of a brain tumor. Learning Corporation of America, 1350 Avenue of the Americas, New York, NY 10019; color; 99 minutes; 1976.

42. *Death, Drugs and Walter* (HS, A). The protagonist of this story is a 12-year-old heroin addict. His short and unhappy career is followed to the end, to the toilet in a Harlem tenement where, wearing a Snoopy T-shirt, he finally overdosed. Interviews with Walter's grieving aunt and his friends raise many points for discussion about the dangers of drugs, the unmet needs of children, and the kind of society in which this sort of thing can happen. Viewfinders, Inc., Box 1665, Evanston, IL 60204; color film; 13 minutes.

43. *Death Education* (HS). George Daugherty, author of a variety of death education materials for school use, talks about different courses already implemented in grade and high schools. Excerpts from various visual presentations used in those courses are shown. Allied Memorial Council, P.O. Box 30112, Seattle, WA 98103; color videotape or film; 30 minutes.

44. *Death: How Can You Live With It?* (GS, HS). This 19-

minute clip from the Walt Disney film *Napoleon and Samantha* focuses on the reaction of a young boy to the dying of his grandfather. The producers believe the film would be effective in triggering discussion, a guide for which is included. Walt Disney Educational Media Company, 500 S. Buena Vista St., Burbank, CA 91521; color; 19 minutes; 1977.

45. *Death in Literature* (HS, A). This program presents a great variety of literature, from Psalm 104 and Ecclesiastes through Shakespeare to John Gunther, Tom Stoppard, and Simone de Beauvoir. Commentary introduces each piece of literature and its historical and cultural context. In addition, certain themes like the loss of friends and suicide are developed in the literary selections. Guidance Associates, Communications Park, Box 300, White Plains, NY 10603; two color filmstrips and audiocassettes or records; teacher's guide.

46. *Death in the Family* (A). Eda LeShan, author of *Learning to Say Goodby,* discusses the pain and the grief of survivors. Children, too, experience great suffering. Ms. LeShan analyzes their emotions and suggests ways of helping them cope. Psychology Today Cassettes, P.O. Box 278, Pratt Station, Brooklyn, NY 11205; audiocassette.

47. *Death of a Gandy Dancer* (HS, A). This brilliant little film story explores how the dying of Grandfather Ben affects other members of the Matthews family. Ben's daughter and son-in-law are concerned and loving, but both want to hide the truth. Grandson Josh is the focal point of Ben's last days and, as it turns out, the best hope that the grandfather's principles and ideals will live on in his progeny. Casting and acting are superb, and the story is rich in insight for students of death education. Family dynamics in the dying trajectory, the importance of memory and progeny, truth telling, and the advantages of choosing one's manner of dying are just a few topics that discussion can explore. Learning Corporation of America, 1350 Avenue of the Americas, New York, NY 10019; color; 26 minutes; 1977.

48. *Death of a Newborn* (A, P). Presented in this program is an

interview with a young couple who lost their firstborn infant at age four weeks. Valuable insights are offered into parental needs, problems, grief and mourning, and into intervention techniques that do and do not work. Polymorph Films, 118 South St., Boston, MA 02111; color film or videotape; 32 minutes; brochure; 1976.

49. *Death of a Sibling* (A). Beginning with an actual case of a child's accidental death in a house fire, the film portrays and interviews the parents as they struggle to tell the surviving sibling and work through their fears, guilt, and other emotions. Then two physicians review these events and generalize about anticipated emotional and other problems in such cases, questions for care givers to expect, and what methods of helping would be most appropriate. Network for Continuing Medical Education, 15 Columbus Circle, New York, NY 10023; color videotape; 19 minutes; 1972.

50. *Death of the Wished-for Child* (A). Dr. Glen W. Davidson, Professor of Thanatology at Southern Illinois University School of Medicine, interviews a mother who lost a wished-for child at birth and who developed emotional problems because of errors in intervention made by her care givers. Davidson makes quite clear what should be done and said in such situations. OGR Service Corporation, P.O. Box 3586, Springfield, IL 62708; color film; 28 minutes.

51. *Death Themes in Literature* (HS). See *Perspectives on Death: A Thematic Teaching Unit.*

52. *Death Themes in Music* (HS). See *Perspectives on Death: A Thematic Teaching Unit.*

53. *Death through the Eyes of the Artist* (HS). Presented on this 87-frame color filmstrip are photographs of masterpieces of world art treating death in various ways. Audiocassette commentary analyzes the themes of death illustrated in each work and generalizes about the universality of death and its portrayal in art. Educational Perspectives Associates, P.O. Box 213, DeKalb, IL 60115; see also *Perspectives on Death: A Thematic Teaching Unit.*

54. *Depression/Suicide: You Can Turn Bad Feelings into Good Ones* (HS, A). The subject of this film is teen-age suicide.

Young people who have attempted suicide are interviewed, and they explain what motivated them. They now successfully control remaining suicidal urges and are putting their lives back in order. University of California at Berkeley, Extension Media Center, 2223 Fulton St., Berkeley, CA 94720; color; 28 minutes; 1976.

55. *Dying Child* (A). Dr. Elisabeth Kübler-Ross addresses herself in this videotaped lecture to the problems and needs of dying children, their parents and care givers. She offers several specific suggestions on ways of getting children to express their feelings about their deaths: poetry, play therapy, and art activities, for example. Medical College of South Carolina, Division of Continuing Education, 80 Barre St., Charleston, SC 29401; color; 42 minutes; 1975.

56. *The Dying Patient and his Family* (A). Presentations by four experts at a critical-care medicine symposium were recorded: Dr. P. G. Gaffney, "The Dying Child"; Dr. Ned Cassem, "The Dying Adult"; Ms. Margaret Wynn, "The Social Worker's Role"; and Rev. G. E. Jackson, "The Clergyman's Role." University of Pittsburgh, School of Medicine, 1022 H. Scaife Hall, Pittsburgh, PA 15261; four audiocassettes; 1974.

57. *Emily: The Story of a Mouse* (GS). A simple story designed to introduce the concept of death at the elementary level, the film tells the life of a field mouse growing from a child to an adult, raising her children, then dying. Even in her death, life goes on, for her body provides warmth and nourishment for new life. Viewfinders, Inc., Box 1665, Evanston, IL 60204; 5 minutes; 1975.

58. *Emotional Support for Dying Patients* (A). Dr. Jimmie Holland lectures on common attitudes toward and conceptions of death and provides helpful suggestions for dealing with dying children and their families. Communications in Learning, 2280 Main St., Buffalo, NY 14214; audiocassette and slides; 38 minutes.

59. *Epitaph: The Lingering Heart* (HS, A). A young father is diagnosed as having leukemia, approaches his death, and dies within 15 months. At the same time, the film studies his wife and daughters and records their grief, bereavement,

then readjustment to a new life. WKYC-TV, Public Affairs Department, 1403 E. Sixth St., Cleveland, OH 44114; color; 25 minutes; 1975.

60. *Explaining Death to Children* (A). Rabbi Earl Grollman, who has written extensively on this subject, offers essential introductory concepts. Available from Allied Memorial Council, P.O. Box 30112, Seattle, WA 98103; color film or videotape; 30 minutes; 1974.

61. *Extending Life* (MS, HS). This brief survey of the moral and social implications of scientific advances in "life extension" would be useful to introduce the topic to school children. BFA Educational Media, 2211 Michigan Ave., Santa Monica, CA 90404; color film; 15 minutes; 1976.

62. *The Family of the Dying Patient* (A, P). Nationally known nursing consultant Virginia Barckley addresses an audience of nurses, though all care givers will find her remarks useful. She observes that the families of dying patients must be well understood, too, and handled with the same thoughtful care as the patients. Different problems arise when the dying person is a child, a parent, or an aged spouse. Whatever the case, family members have particular needs influenced by lifestyles and family customs. A number of positive suggestions are offered. American Cancer Society, 777 Third Ave., New York, NY 10017; 23 minutes; discussion guide; 1972.

63. *Family Reactions to Stillbirth* (P). This lecture-presentation urges medical professionals to deal more sympathetically with such situations and offers useful background information and suggestions. Communications in Learning, 2280 Main St., Buffalo, NY 14214; audiocassette; 16 minutes.

64. *Father* (HS, A). Starring Burgess Meredith, this fine little film is based on a short story by Anton Chekhov. Ned Kelly, a hansom cab driver in New York's Central Park, alone in the world since the recent death of his son, tries to share his grief with passengers in his cab but is coldly rebuffed or ignored. The point is made beautifully but painfully that grief must be shared. University of California at Berkeley, Extension Media Center, 2223 Fulton St., Berkeley, CA 94720; black and white; 1971.

65. *Feelings of a Father* (A). A father discusses his grief at the loss of his child. The Compassionate Friends, P.O. Box 1347, Oak Brook, IL 60521; audiocassette.

66. *The Following Sea* (HS, A). At the funeral of his father, an old fisherman, Charles recalls his father's life and realizes the legacy of wisdom and insight left behind, which now, like a following sea, continues to move the lives of his survivors. McGraw-Hill Films, 1221 Avenue of the Americas, New York, NY 10020; black and white film; 11 minutes.

67. *Gale is Dead* (A). A 19-year-old girl dies of a heroin overdose, and this award-winning documentary film attempts to reveal the causes of her addiction, not simply the effects. Framed at beginning and end by scenes from her funeral, the film interviews teachers and acquaintances, explores her early years and formative experiences, and suggests that in many ways society and its institutions, not simply the addict's own psychological condition, are at least partly to blame; they could have done more for her. Time-Life Films, Time-Life Building, 1271 Avenue of the Americas, New York, NY 10020; 51 minutes; 1970.

68. *The Garden Party* (HS, A). Based on the Katherine Mansfield short story, the film juxtaposes upper- and lower-class attitudes, assumptions, misinformation, and fears about death and postdeath rituals, as it portrays in depth the effects of death on a young girl. This is excellent for discussion purposes. Paramount Communications, 5451 Marathon St., Hollywood, CA 90038; 24 minutes.

69. *Graduation Day* (HS, A). A probation officer manages to help a suicidal teen-ager back to a healthy sense of reality. The point is made that a worthwhile life must be based on a sense of personal identity and inner freedom. Paulist Productions, P.O. Box 1057, Pacific Palisades, CA 90272; color film; 27 minutes; 1973.

70. *Grief Therapy* (A). Originally produced as part of the CBS-TV "60 Minutes" series, this film presents several on-camera grief therapy sessions. Dr. Donald Ramsey leads a mother to "let go," to face the facts and separate herself from her daughter, whose accidental death she has been mourning intensely for over 2½ years. Insights into the

nature of grief are graphically presented. Carousel Films, 1501 Broadway, New York, NY 10036; color; 20 minutes; 1976.

71. *Handling Holidays* (A). The title refers to the special problem faced by parents wo have lost a child, and this audiocassette offers practical advice from people who have had the experience. The Compassionate Friends, P.O. Box 1347, Oak Brook, IL 60521.

72. *Help Me! The Story of a Teenage Suicide* (HS, A). Based on the story of one young girl who becomes a suicide statistic, this film explores behavior patterns of suicide-prone people and offers suggestions for effective intervention. S.L. Film Productions, P.O. Box 41108, Los Angeles, CA 90041; color; 25 minutes.

73. *How Death Came to Earth* (MS, HS, A). For classes interested in the cross-cultural study of death, this well-made little film with attractive musical accompaniment may be valuable. It retells an East Indian folk tale about a time when there were two suns and two moons and no one died. When one of each pair fell in love with each other and came to play on earth, people were afraid of the fire, so a hunter was sent to kill them both. Thereupon storms, rain, and death descended upon the earth. McGraw-Hill Films, 1221 Avenue of the Americas, New York, NY 10020; color; 14 minutes; 1971.

74. *How Do You Explain Death to Children?* (HS, A). Use of this film is free to classroom teachers and death educators. Write for information and make booking well ahead of time. Walter J. Klein Co., Ltd., 6301 Carmel Rd., Box 220766, Charlotte, NC 28222; color; 28 minutes; 1976.

75. *I Never Saw Another Butterfly* (A). This is a film record of a fascinating set of children's drawings, which include depictions of the happiness and joy of houses, toys, and flowers as well as vivid renderings of funeral scenes and death by gallows and lightning. What is special are the artists, inmates of a Nazi concentration camp in World War II. Macmillan Films, 34 MacQuesten Parkway South, Mount Vernon, NY 10550; color; 15 minutes.

76. *Just Hold My Hand* (A, P). Two middle-aged women, both

dying of cancer, are filmed during the last six months of their lives. One is a widow, a mother of seven, whose "most horrifying thought is having to leave my family." Pressures, problems, and conflicts in the family group and in the individual children are revealed. The other woman, a professional research biologist, is especially troubled by her inability to work and the concomitant (for her) loss of human dignity; thus she decides to stop her chemotherapy treatments. Both women discuss euthanasia at some length. The mother of seven would never consider interfering with the plan of God, but the scientist disagrees: "I say I'll never do it, but I know it's in my medicine cabinet. Maybe I will. . . . " The overall theme of this impressive and very moving filmed documentary is how two people overcome great odds to live their last months meaningfully. Doctors Ned Cassem and Melvin Krant, involved in the care of these patients, comment. Write Mr. Howard Finkelstein, Boston Broadcasters, Inc., 5 TV Place, Needham Br., Boston, MA 02190; color videotape; 60 minutes.

77. *Last Rites: A Child's Reaction to Death* (MS, HS, A). At his mother's funeral, a young boy cannot grasp the meaning and the reality of his loss. He retreats into fantasy until a stranger is able to get through and to help the boy accept. This new film on "the mystery of death and its incomprehensibility to a child" has been described as an excellent teaching tool. Filmakers Library, 133 E. 58th St., Suite 703 A, New York, NY 10022; color; 30 minutes; 1979.

78. *Leukemia Panel Discussion* (A). Parents of leukemic children and their doctors discuss the psychological and emotional effects of the disease on the families. Stanford University, School of Medicine, Division of Instructional Media, M 207, Stanford, CA 94305; color videotape; 32 minutes; 1975.

79. *The Life That's Left* (A). A number of people who have experienced a loss—an elderly widower, a young widow, a sibling, parents, and the mother of a stillborn baby—describe their feelings in interviews. Great Plains National Instructional Television Library, Box 80669, Lincoln, NE 68501; color film or videotape; 29 minutes.

80. *The Magic Moth* (HS, A). Based on the book by Virginia

Lee, the film portrays the illness, death, and funeral of Maryanne, the middle child of five, and the reactions of her family and friends. The family is a model (perhaps somewhat unrealistic) of healthy relationships characterized by open discussion and honest acceptance of the reality of death. Their frankly stated Christian beliefs and point of view may be objected to by some as simplistic. As Maryanne dies, the beautiful moth of the title springs from a cocoon given to her earlier by her brother. The acting is, at times, only fair. Centron Educational Films, P.O. Box 687, 1621 W. Ninth St., Lawrence, KA 66044; color; 22 minutes; 1977.

81. *Marek* (A). Marek is a seven-year-old boy who must undergo dangerous cardiac surgery to correct a birth defect. The doctors advise the parents of the risks involved and counsel the family attentively. The surgery is performed, but there are complications and Marek dies. The parents are then helped through the shock of the loss. Produced by BBC-TV, the film is well made and impressive. Time-Life Films, Time-Life Building, 1271 Avenue of the Americas, New York, NY 10020; color; 45 minutes; 1978.

82. *Mongoloid Infant: Should We Operate?* (A, P). A panel of doctors at the University of Virginia Medical School breaks this question down into its more specific medical and ethical components and discusses the varying types and prognoses of mongoloidism, the "quality of life" concept, and the extent of parental rights in determining treatment. University of Virginia, School of Medicine, Charlottesville, VA 22904; black-and-white videotape; 60 minutes; 1973.

83. *My Grandson Lew* (MS, HS, A). When, how, and what to tell children about a death in the family are questions raised by this film, based on the book by Charlotte Zolotow. Lew is thinking about his grandfather and wonders when he will visit again. Mother tells Lew that the grandfather died and that she was afraid to tell him earlier because he was too young. They then share happy memories of grandfather. Barr Films, P.O. Box 5667, 3490 E. Foothill Blvd., Pasadena, CA 91107; color; 13 minutes; 1976.

84. *My Son, Kevin* (A). Kevin, a "thalidomide baby," has no

arms or legs, but he rises above misfortune to attend a community school and be a loved and loving person. This film would interest discussion groups on policies and attitudes toward malformed fetuses, abortion, and birth defects. Viewfinders, Inc., Box 1665, Evanston, IL 60204; color; 24 minutes.

85. *My Turtle Died Today* (GS). The book on which this cartoon is based tells the story of a pet turtle getting sick, dying, then being mourned by three children until they realize that life continues. BFA Educational Media, 2211 Michigan Ave., Santa Monica, CA 90404; color film; 5 minutes.

86. *A Need to Know: A Family Faces Death* (A, P). Part of the video tape series "Interventions in Family Therapy," this program presents an interview between Lois Jaffe, M.S.W., a leukemia patient herself, and the family of a child with the same disease. ETL Video Publishers, 1170 Commonwealth Ave., Boston, MA 02134; color; 60 minutes; 1975.

87. *Nine-year-olds Talk about Death* (GS, HS, A). School teachers and others interested in understanding children's attitudes toward death will find this short film informative and stimulating. The format is straightforward. A group of fourth graders are filmed as they answer questions about death posed by a teacher who is off-camera and comment on one another's responses. Here is yet another valuable illustration of the sometimes profound wisdom of children. International Film Bureau, 332 S. Michigan Ave., Chicago, IL 60604; black and white; 15 minutes; 1977.

88. *Nursing Management of Children with Cancer* (A, P). The purpose of this film is to illustrate the skills, commitment, and rewards involved in pediatric cancer nursing. The procedures demonstrated include infusions, mouth care, control of infections and fevers, ostomy care, and play therapy. The need for emotional support for patients and their families is explained, as is the nurse's teaching responsibility in aiding parents to help and treat their children at home. Statistical information is provided that suggests that the prognosis of many childhood cancers is improving. American Cancer

Society, 777 Third Ave., New York, NY 10017; color; 22 minutes; 1974.

89. *One in 350: Sudden Infant Death* (A). Perhaps one of the most serious problems faced by parents who have lost a child to SIDS is the tactless ignorance of family, friends, and well-meaning care givers. Education on the nature of the disease and on the fact that so little is known about it, can help parents and the public alike. In this film, parents share their experiences and their particular kind of grief. National SIDS Foundation, Room 1904, 310 S. Michigan Ave., Chicago, IL 60604; black and white; 30 minutes.

90. *Parents and the Dying Child* (A, P). Eugenia Waechter, a counselor of dying children and their families, describes the principles she follows in her practice and the lessons she has learned. Big Sur Recordings, P.O. Box 91, Big Sur, CA 93920; audiocassette; 90 minutes; 1974.

91. *Perspectives on Death: A Thematic Teaching Unit* (HS). Widely used in secondary schools, this program consists of an anthology of readings, a student activity book, teacher's resource book, and four audiovisuals. "Funeral Customs around the World" (a 110-frame color filmstrip and audio-cassette) is a cross-cultural survey. "Death through the Eyes of the Artist" (an 87-frame color filmstrip and audio-cassette) shows the work of such masters as Michelangelo, Rembrandt, Bosch, and Picasso and explains how style, color, and symbolism can "capture the face and mood of death." Narrators read from selected works of Shakespeare, Poe, London, Wilder, and others in "Death Themes in Literature" (audiocassette, 20 minutes); and musical selections like "Danse Macabre," Mozart's "Requiem," "Die Erl-Konig" by Schubert, "Taps," and "Deep River" are played in "Death Themes in Music" (audiocassette, 18 minutes). Components of the unit are available separately. Educational Perspectives Associates, P.O. Box 213, DeKalb, IL 60115.

92. *Physician's Role with the Dying Patient* (P). Three programs make up this series aimed at helping practicing physicians improve their work with dying patients. "Children Die Too" offers suggestions on treating dying children and relating

effectively with family members. "Maintaining Integrity of the Profession" offers guidelines for physician-patient exchange at various stages in the dying process. "The Philosophy of Dying" discusses legal, social, and emotional factors in the dying situation. University of Arizona, Health Sciences Center, Division of Biomedical Communications, Tucson, AZ 85724; three color videotapes; 50-57 minutes each; 1974.

93. *Poetry of Death* (HS, A). A number of well-known poetic treatments of death, ranging from Shakespeare to contemporary song lyrics and including such chestnuts as Robert Louis Stevenson's "Requiem" and William Cullen Bryant's "Thanatopsis," are read to the accompaniment of guitar music and evocative photographs. Spectrum Educational Media, 105 Beverly Ave., Morton, IL 61550; two color filmstrips and audiocassettes, with text; 1974.

94. *A Question of Values* (A). Down's syndrome (DS) is explained, and moral issues related to keeping and caring for Down's syndrome and other handicapped infants are raised. Patients (three infants and three children, aged 5-21) and their families are introduced to illustrate commentary on the widely varying physical and psychological traits found in the DS population. This presentation tries to counter the film *Who Should Survive?* which presents the case of a DS infant, unwanted by parents, who was allowed to die without corrective surgery. Edward Feil Productions, 4614 Prospect Ave., Cleveland, OH 44103; color film; 28 minutes; 1972.

95. *Rabbit* (GS, HS, A). A 9-year-old boy learns that taking care of three pet rabbits given as an Easter present is more of a chore than he thought. Finding homes for two of them, he releases the third in the woods and then is filled with sadness and guilt when he discovers it dead. His first encounter with death is complicated by the burden of responsibility. The film is a sensitive, insightful portrait of the child's responses to loss and death. Viewfinders, Inc., Box 1665, Evanston, IL 60204; color; 15 minutes; 1974.

96. *Reactions of Children to Serious Illness, Death, and Natural Catastrophe* (P). This is a videotaped lecture to a medical

audience by Dr. Howard Hansen. University of Washington Audiovisual Services, Seattle, WA 98195; 60 minutes.

97. *Reinvestment-Reorganization-Recovery* (A). The words outline a program of therapeutic action for parents who have lost a child. The Compassionate Friends, P.O. Box 1347, Oak Brook, IL 60521; audiocassette.

98. *Richie* (HS, A). The theme of this story is teen-age drug addiction and its impact on a family. Richie's parents cannot comprehend his increasing dependency on drugs and his resulting behavior changes. Disintegrating communication results in increasingly hostile confrontations in the home, climaxing in the father's shooting of Richie. This program is an edited selection from the feature film *The Death of Richie,* based on a book by Thomas Thompson. Learning Corporation of America, 1350 Avenue of the Americas, New York, NY 10019; color film; 31 minutes; 1978.

99. *Rick: An Adolescent Suicide* (A). A 17-year-old high school senior committed suicide. The film tries to recreate events and to investigate Rick's mental and emotional state before the fact. Medical Media Network, Room 514, 10995 LeConte Ave., Los Angeles, CA 90024; black and white; 29 minutes; 1969.

100. *The Role of the Schools in Death Education* (A). Schools at all levels should offer death education, argues Dr. Dan Leviton. He offers specific commentary on curricula as well as teacher and parent preparation in the subject matter, which should include crisis intervention. The Charles Press, Bowie, MD 20715; audiocassette; 27 minutes.

101. *Ronnie's Tune* (GS, HS). The film is a carefully detailed, realistic portrait of complex family reactions following the death of a teen-age son. Only with painful difficulty is it revealed to a visiting niece, Julie, that her cousin Ronnie's death was a suicide and that Ronnie's father has left his wife as a result. Ronnie's mother makes a great effort and is finally willing to talk freely about her response to the death and to share her grief. After tears, grieving, and much thought of her own, Julie decides to learn to play

Ronnie's banjo. Wombat Productions, Little Lake, Glendale Road, P.O. Box 70, Ossining, NY 10562; color; 18 minutes; 1978.

102. *Sandcastle* (GS, MS). This program for ages 10–12 presents a conversation between a father and his children on the unexpected death of their mother. Image Publications, Miles-Samuelson, Inc., 15 E. 26th St., New York, NY 10010; color filmstrip and audiocassette or record; 1971.

103. *A Small Statistic* (A). This film records the reactions of a young couple to the death of their first child. Association Instructional Materials, 866 Third Ave., New York, NY 10022; color; 27 minutes. (Recent correspondence with the distributor indicates that the film is now "withdrawn from circulation by sponsor.")

104. *Some Days It's Harder To Say Yes: Suicide in the Classroom* (HS). Offered here are interviews with two high school students who are suicidal, together with related information and insight into teens and suicide. Highly Specialized Promotions, 391 Atlantic Ave., Brooklyn, NY 11201; color videotape; 30 minutes; teacher's guide; 1979.

105. *A Special Kind of Care* (A). This film has two main purposes: (1) to dramatize the effects on a family of a mother slowly dying of cancer and the related problems of truth telling and (2) to highlight the nature and functions of the National Cancer Foundation and its service arm, Cancer Care, Inc. With the counseling of Cancer Care, the father is finally able to meet the needs of his children and of himself in the crisis situation. Association Films, 866 Third Ave., New York, NY 10022; color; 14 minutes; 1968.

106. *The Street* (HS, A). Mordecai Richler's fine little book is turned into a delightfully moving animated film. A grandmother dies slowly in her son's home; and the family, especially her grandchildren, reacts to her passing. The urban poor, ethnic Jewish atmosphere is faithfully reproduced. A nine-year-old grandson, loving but totally realistic and irrepressible, provides the main point of view. Living and dying in this family are real, ordinary, serious, and comic. These are individual people beautifully portrayed,

experiencing death in their own way. National Film Board of Canada, 16th Floor, 1251 Avenue of the Americas, New York, NY 10020; color; 10 minutes.

107. *Sudden Infant Death Syndrome* (A). A brief introduction to the topic. National Audiovisual Center, Order Section, Washington, D.C. 20409; color film; 4 minutes; 1976.

108. *Sudden Infant Death Syndrome and the Pediatrician* (P). Directed at physicians, this program presents guidelines for working with parents of SIDS-prone children, reports on recent research into the syndrome, and surveys parental responses to SIDS deaths. University of Arizona, Health Sciences Center, Division of Biomedical Communications, Tucson, AZ 85724; color videotape; 43 minutes; 1974.

109. *Suicide: Causes and Prevention* (HS, A). This presentation for a high school audience includes issues and case studies carefully presented to foster discussion. Sunburst Communications, 39 Washington Ave., Pleasantville, NY 10570; two color filmstrips and audiocassettes or records; teacher's guide; 1976.

110. *Suicides: Causes and Prevention* (A). Suicide among high school and college students is the focus of these two programs. Causal factors and varying scholarly theories about them are treated in the first program. In the second, the emphasis is on prevention and intervention. Human Relations Media Center, 41 Washington Ave., Pleasantville, NY 10570; two color filmstrips with audiocassettes or records.

111. *Suicide: Who Will Cry for Me?* (HS, A). This new sound filmstrip set focuses on the growing problem of teen-age suicide. It surveys and corrects a number of myths about suicide, analyzes reasons why the teen-age population is particularly at risk, offers detailed analysis of warning signs, and in general offers much useful information for teens themselves and for parents and care givers. Learning Arts, P.O. Box 179, Wichita, KS 67201; three color filmstrips and audiocassettes; teachers guide; 1979.

112. *The Syndrome of Ordinary Grief* (A, P). In an interview, a sophomore medical student describes his reactions to the accidental death of his only child, a two-year-old boy,

some weeks earlier. Included is a scholarly paper on this case history. University of Texas Medical Branch, Video-tape Library of Clinical Psychiatric Syndromes, Galveston, TX 77550; color videotape; 32 minutes.

113. *Talking to Children About Death* (A). Dr. George C. Williams argues that of course children should be taught about death. They almost automatically adopt parents' attitudes, so parents must straighten themselves out and then share openly with children. Otherwise children may have emotional problems in later life. Concrete suggestions for parents are offered. The Charles Press, Bowie, MD 20715; audiocassette; 57 minutes; 1972.

114. *A Taste of Blackberries* (MS). See *Understanding Death Series*.

115. *Teen-age Suicide: A National Epidemic* (A). Joseph Teicher lectures. Psychology Today Cassettes, P.O. Box 278, Pratt Station, Brooklyn, NY 11205; audiocassette; 1977.

116. *Terminal* (A). Members of the Open Theatre Ensemble of New York City perform in a frankly experimental production that combines acting, dancing, chanting, and panto-mime. The theme is death and a wide variety of related issues, attitudes, and customs. Funeral ritual and hospital treatment of patients, for example, come in for a good measure of satire. Courses approaching death through literature and the other arts or through philosophy or psychology will find this useful. Foundation of Thanatol-ogy, 630 W. 168th St., New York, NY 10032; black-and-white videotape; 30 minutes; 1970.

117. *That Undiscovered Country* (HS). The country "from whose bourn no traveler returns," as Hamlet tells us, is death. The audiocassette portion of this program presents readings of seven popular poetic interpretations of death, with muscial background. An accompanying booklet con-tains these texts and other classic literary statements on death and dying. A detailed teacher's guide with many suggestions for use is included. Perfection Form Company, 1000 N. Second Ave., Logan, IA 51546; audiocassette; reader; teacher's guide.

118. *Themes in Literature: Death* (HS, A). Professional readings

from many authors—Chaucer, Shakespeare, Donne, Boswell, Gray, Wordsworth, Browning, Tolstoy, Dickinson, Synge, Millay, Gunther, Steinbeck, Agee, Stoppard—demonstrate a multiplicity of attitudes to human mortality. Guidance Associates, Communications Park, Box 300, White Plains, NY 10603; two color filmstrips and audiocassettes or records.

119. *Things in Their Season* (HS, A). Members of the Gerlach family, working a dairy farm in southern Wisconsin, were growing apart until the day that wife Peg was diagnosed as having leukemia. In the face of this tragedy the family forced itself back together, facing truth, finally speaking the unspoken, reevaluating their relationships, and eventually finding a measure of happiness. This is a fine film portrayal of the dynamics of death in the family situation. Learning Corporation of America, 1350 Avenue of the Americas, New York, NY 10019; color; 79 minutes; 1975.

120. *To Be Aware of Death* (HS, A). This film surveys a number of young people on their feelings about death and their experiences with it. The commentary is made more attractive by means of accompanying color photography, still pictures, and folk music. University of Minnesota, AV Library Service, 3300 University Ave. S.E., Minneapolis, MN 55414; color; 13 minutes; 1974.

121. *Two Daughters* (A). In this evocative Swedish film, a mother mourns the death of her young daughter and remembers her own mother's death. This is a fine study of relationships and of generations and an effective stimulus to discussion. University of California at Berkeley, Extension Media Center, 2223 Fulton St., Berkeley, CA 94720; color; 22 minutes; 1976.

122. *Uncle Monty's Gone* (GS). Fat Albert and the Cosby Kids react to the death of someone close. Undine's Uncle Monty, a long-time entertainer, agrees to help the kids stage a fund-raising show. When he dies suddenly, Undine is crushed and angrily withdraws from her friends. Then her mother tells her more about Uncle Monty, his zest for life, and how he would have wanted them all to live with enthusiasm and joy. The show must go on, and with

Undine and her friends back together, it does. University of Illinois, Visual Aids Service, 1325 S. Oak St., Champaign, IL 61820; color film; 16 minutes; 1976.

123. *Understanding Changes in the Family: Playing Dead* (GS, MS). This one of a series of filmstrip programs asks an audience of children to role-play. In the process, someone recalls the death of a grandfather, and discussion takes up the idea. Guidance Associates, Communications Park, Box 300, White Plains, NY 10603; color filmstrip and audiocassette or record; 5 minutes.

124. *Understanding Death: A Basic Program in Death and Dying* (MS, HS). Six filmstrips and three accompanying audiocassettes make up this introductory series on the subject for the schools. "Thinking about Death" gives general background and encourages students to examine their own experiences with and attitudes toward death. "Mourning," the second filmstrip, discusses grief as a normal human emotion, and one not exclusively associated with death. "Practical Guidelines," the next program, explains death certificates, wills, organ bequests, and so on. "Death's Moment and the Time that Follows" explains why "death" is so difficult to define in precise medical and legal terms and that scientific advances constantly force changes in society's conception of death and of life. The fifth program, "Dying Occurs in Stages," builds on the theories of Kübler-Ross. Finally, "The Gift of Life" examines various types of "symbolic immortality" and argues that a well-spent life can rob death of some of its sting. Eye Gate Media, 146-01 Archer Ave., Jamaica, NY 11435; six color filmstrips (about 50 frames each) and three audiocassettes, available as a set or singly; 1976.

125. *Understanding Death Series* (MS). Included in this series are four programs especially designed for middle school students, with an accompanying program for parents and teachers. In "Life-Death," death is presented as a natural part of the life cycle; natural, too, are feelings of grief. Causes of death and a number of other topics are covered. In both "Exploring the Cemetery" and "Facts about Funerals," a boy pays visits and gets background informa-

tion from, respectively, a cemeterian and a funeral director. The fourth program, "A Taste of Blackberries," is adapted from a book by Doris Buchanan Smith. A boy loses his best friend, then works through his grief to an awareness of death as a natural part of the human experience. Finally, "Children and Death: A Guide for Parents and Teachers" offers advice on truth telling, death education, the changing stages and levels of children's understanding of death, and other matters. Educational Perspectives Associates, P.O. Box 213, DeKalb, IL 60115; five color filmstrips and audiocassettes, also available separately.

126. *Very Good Friends* (MS, HS, A). When her 11-year-old sister dies suddenly, a 13-year-old is tortured by grief, anger, and guilt. Her parents help her sort through her feelings, accept the loss, and rest more comfortably with her memories. This fine study of a death in the family can stimulate discussion. Learning Corporation of America, 1350 Avenue of the Americas, New York, NY 10019; color film; 20 minutes; 1977.

127. *Walk in the World for Me* (A, P). See *Death and Dying: Closing the Circle.*

128. *Warrendale* (A). This documentary film is mainly the study of an institution for emotionally disturbed children, but its conclusion is of particular interest to death educators. One of the cooks at the institution, a favorite of the children, dies suddenly and unexpectedly. The children's grief reactions are astounding, from angry self-destructive activities to severe depression. Here are many aspects of grief that, in "normal" people, often do not surface or that appear in more "acceptable" guises. Film Division of Grove Press, 53 E. 11th, New York, NY 10003; 105 minutes.

129. *Where is Dead* (A). A six-year-old girl, grieving at the accidental death of her brother, comes to understand death as part of the cycle of life and can then be happy with her memories of her brother. The film is a fine study in the dynamics of grief, especially in the child. While the reactions of the adult family members are not emphasized, the adult-child relationships surrounding the death are

healthy. The acting and the whole production are first
rate. Encyclopaedia Britannica Educational Corporation,
425 N. Michigan Ave., Chicago, IL 60611; color; 19
minutes.

130. *Who Should Survive?* (A). The film opens with the birth of
a baby, a diagnosis of Down's syndrome, the parents'
refusal to permit life-saving abdominal surgery, and the
subsequent starvation of the infant in the hospital. A
19-minute panel discussion then argues various legal, ethical, and scientific aspects of the case. A teacher's guide
and bibliography are available. University of California at
Berkeley, Extension Media Center, 2223 Fulton St., Berkeley, CA 94720; color; 26 minutes; 1972.

131. *Who Speaks for the Baby?* (A). The case of a newborn
mongoloid infant who will die without corrective surgery is
dramatized here. When the parents refuse their consent,
the physician seeks a court order to operate. In a panel
discussion, professionals offer their responses to the question of the title. See also *A Question of Values* and *Who
Should Survive?* Network for Continuing Medical Education, 15 Columbus Circle, New York, NY 10023; color
videotape.

132. *With His Playclothes On* (A, P). At 21 months, Jerry dies
suddenly of causes that, even after autopsy, are not
completely understood. The immediate emotional responses of the parents and three older brothers are vividly
presented. Two months after the death, the family is still
torn by unresolved shock, anger, and conflict, as the
family members react on different levels and from incom-
pletely shared points of view. This study of grief in the
family, one of the best available on the subject, includes
extensive analytical commentary by Dr. Glen Davidson,
Professor and Chief of Thanatology, Department of Psychi-
atry, Southern Illinois University School of Medicine. OGR
Service Corporation, P.O. Box 3586, Springfield, IL 62708;
color filmstrip and audiocassette; 47 minutes; 1976.

133. *You Are Not Alone* (A). SIDS is the topic of this program.
Parents who have lost children to the disease, care givers,
and general audiences are reminded that causes of the

syndrome are largely unknown and that little can be done to prevent an attack. Specific advice is offered on dealing with emotional and other responses of parents, siblings, relatives, and friends. The cases of several couples are dramatized. National SIDS Foundation, Room 1904, 310 S. Michigan Ave., Chicago, IL 60604; color film; 25 minutes; 1976.

134. *The Young Man and Death* (HS, A). Unique among audiovisual materials on death is this ballet danced to music of J. S. Bach by Rudolph Nureyev and Zizi Jeanmaire. The ballerina in the role of Death acts alternately as a destroyer and as a temptress. The Young Man, first fleeing, then falling victim to her blandishments, gives himself up to her. Having won her victory, she scornfully turns away from him and offers him a noose. This film would be very effective in classes studying death in the arts or as a stimulus to discussion. Macmillan Films, 34 MacQuesten Parkway South, Mount Vernon, NY 10550; color; 16 minutes; 1976.

135. *You See—I've Had a Life* (HS, A). At 13, Paul Hendricks is diagnosed as having leukemia. After some initial attempts at denial, the parents decide to tell Paul. The whole family shares the experience with him, working to enhance the quality of his life in the time remaining. The film records Paul's continuing school and athletic activities, treatments by medical staff, the care-giving activities, and the personal reactions of the parents and of Paul himself. This is a moving, well-made story of one family's togetherness in the face of death and of one child's courage. The words of the title, which accurately suggest the essence of his character and the quality of his response to death, are spoken by Paul to reassure a friend who came to offer sympathy. Viewfinders, Inc., Box 1665, Evanston, IL 60204; black and white; 32 minutes; 1973.

136. *The Youth Killers* (MS, HS). Leading causes of death in this age group are discussed in this program. A teacher's guide is included. Audiovisual Narrative Arts, Box 398, Pleasantville, NY 10570; two color filmstrips and audiocassettes or records; 1975.

Appendix

The Compassionate Friends (A). The history, goals, and operating methods of this self-help organization for bereaved parents are introduced. The Compassionate Friends, P.O. Box 1347, Oak Brook, IL 60521; color filmstrip and audiocassette; 1980.

I Want to Die (HS, A). At a Thanksgiving dinner, Bill, a college student, is deeply depressed; he is going to quit school, he says, and is planning to kill himself. The balance of the film reveals what it is about his relationship with his family that had led to Bill's decisions. At the root is a failure of communication between parents and child. A closing commentary by movie star Kirk Douglas asks viewers to be prepared to help such people. University of Illinois, Visual Aids Service, 1325 S. Oak St., Champaign, IL 61820; color; 27 minutes; 1977.

Preventing Teen Suicide: You Can Help (HS, A). "Jennifer is 16, pretty, bright, popular, talented—and a suicide." This new program first outlines causal factors in Jennifer's decision: the divorce of her parents, her break-up with her boy friend, her rejection by the college of her choice. These are all common enough occurrences, but in this case, because no one heeded danger signals, their cumulative effect was another teen suicide. The program then shows the family, teachers, and friends as they consider what they might have said and done for Jennifer—and lessons are drawn for the viewer. Sunburst Communications, 39 Washington Ave., Pleasantville, NY 10570; three color filmstrips and audiocassettes or records; teachers guide; 1980.

Talking about Death with Children (GS, MS). Rabbi Earl Grollman, an authority on this topic, explains death and the funeral to an audience of children. Batesville Management Services, P.O. Drawer 90, Batesville, IN 47006; color filmstrip and audiocassette; 11 minutes; 1980.

Time to Come Home (A, P). In some situations a dying child is better cared for at home than in the hospital. This film builds on the team concept—physician, nurses, and parents—

but focuses on the instruction of parents as primary care givers. Lessons for physical care of the child are given, and both the benefits and risks of bringing the dying child home are discussed. Department of Physical Medicine and Rehabilitation, University Hospital, 860 Mayo, Box 297, 420 Delaware St. S.E., Minneapolis, MN 55455; color; 24 minutes.

We Can Help (A, P). This film describes a multifaceted family-oriented care-giving program for children with cancer, a program combining medical treatment with personal, academic, and vocational counseling. The patients and their family members are interviewed. Polymorph Films, Inc., 118 South St., Boston, MA 02111; color film or videotape; 20 minutes.

When Disaster Strikes: Coping with Loss, Grief and Rejection (HS, A). Typical human responses to life crises like serious illness, death, and the loss of a loved one are outlined in stages: shock, anger, and acceptance. Variations in individuals are noted, as are related physical and emotional effects. Then coping strategies and grief work are explained, and the complex healing process is clarified. Dramatized illustrations make the subject matter concrete. Sunburst Communications, 39 Washington Ave., Pleasantville, NY 10570; three filmstrips and audiocassettes; teachers guide; 1980.

TOPICAL INDEX TO "AUDIOVISUAL RESOURCES"

Numbers refer to entry numbers.

TITLE INDEX TO "BOOKS FOR CHILDREN"

Numbers refer to page numbers.

189

INDEX